LOST CITIES
AND
VANISHED
CIVILIZATIONS

LOST CITIES

AND

VANISHED

CIVILIZATIONS

ROBERT SILVERBERG

76359

CHILTON BOOK COMPANY

RADNOR, PENNSYLVANIA

Copyright © 1962 by Robert Silverberg
First Edition   *All Rights Reserved*

Second Printing, October 1963
Third Printing, January 1968
Fourth Printing, October 1971
Fifth Printing, December 1973

Published in Radnor, Pa. by Chilton Book Company
and simultaneously in Ontario, Canada
by Thomas Nelson & Sons, Ltd.
Library of Congress Catalog Card Number 62-8846
ISBN   0-8019-0837-X
Designed by William E. Lickfield
Manufactured in the United States of America

Once again, to MY PARENTS

Introduction

Man's exploration of outer space began just a few years ago. But the exploration of *inner* space, below the surface of the Earth, has been going on for hundreds of years. As far back as the time of Plato's Greece, men have dug for the treasures of the past buried in the ground. Today, and for the last 200 years, systematic digging has been and is going on all over the world, as one by one the cities of mankind's yesterdays have come once again to light.

And what wonders the science of archaeology has given us! The Troy of Priam and Hector—the Crete of the dreaded King Minos—the Babylon of Belshazzar and Nebuchadnezzar—all these fabled cities have returned from the land of myth. In Italy an entire Roman city of the time of Emperor Titus has emerged after centuries of burial beneath volcanic ash. From the jungles of Central America has come the world of the Mayas, with its mighty pyramids and towering temples, while half a world away in Cambodia the jungle has been forced to release its grip on Angkor, city of the enigmatic Khmer people.

The story of archaeology is the story of a band of dedicated men, patiently laboring with pick and shovel under blazing suns. Archaeology is sweaty work. It is tiring work. It is slow work. The hours are long, the rewards often few and far between. There is nothing romantic about the day-by-day routine of archaeology.

But romance enters when the archaeologist's labors are done—when another of man's lost cities has returned from ruin and burial. The curtains of time are drawn back, and we see how men lived at the dawn of history. We share in their dreams, in their arts, in their accomplishments—and, ultimately, in their tragedy. For this book is a story of lost cities and vanished civilizations. Each of the six peoples dealt with here had its moment of history, its years of glory, and then passed on into memory.

Into the cities of the dead, then, we go in the chapters to come. The archaeologists have done the work for us. Men named Schliemann and Thompson and Evans have done the spade-work already. The cities of yesterday stand revealed, freed of the encroachments of forest or desert or jungle. The valiant men of archaeology have given us the priceless gift of our own past.

To Pompeii, then, and to Troy, to Crete and to Babylon, to Chichén Itzá and distant Angkor we shall go. And our thanks must go to those explorers of inner space, the archaeologists who toiled to reveal our yesterdays.

Robert Silverberg

Contents

LOST CITIES
AND
VANISHED
CIVILIZATIONS

1

Pompeii

Not very far from Naples a strange city sleeps under the hot Italian sun. It is the city of Pompeii, and there is no other city quite like it in all the world. No one lives in Pompeii but crickets and beetles and lizards, yet every year thousands of people travel from distant countries to visit it.

Pompeii is a dead city. No one has lived there for nearly 2,000 years—not since the summer of the year A.D. 79, to be exact.

Until that year Pompeii was a prosperous city of 25,000 people. Nearby was the Bay of Naples, an arm of the blue Mediterranean. Rich men came down from wealthy Rome, 125 miles to the north, to build luxurious seaside villas. Fertile farmlands occupied the fields surrounding Pompeii. Rising sharply behind the city was the 4,000-foot bulk of Mount Vesuvius, a grass-covered slope where the shepherds of Pompeii took their goats to graze. Pompeii was a busy city and a happy one.

It died suddenly, in a terrible rain of fire and ashes.

The tragedy struck on the 24th of August, A.D. 79. Mount Vesuvius, which had slumbered quietly for centuries, exploded with savage violence. Death struck on a hot summer afternoon. Tons of hot ashes fell on Pompeii, smothering it, hiding it from sight. For three days the sun did not break through the cloud of volcanic ash that filled the sky. And when the eruption ended, Pompeii was buried deep. A thriving city had perished in a single day.

Centuries passed . . . Pompeii was forgotten. Then, 1,500 years later, it was discovered again. Beneath the protecting shroud of ashes, the city lay intact. Everything was as it had been the day Vesuvius erupted. There were still loaves of bread in the ovens of the bakeries. In the wine shops, the wine jars were in place, and on one counter could be seen a stain where a customer had thrown down his glass and fled.

Modern archaeology began with the discovery of buried Pompeii. Before then, the digging of treasures from the ground had been a haphazard and unscholarly affair. But the excavation of Pompeii was done in a systematic, scientific manner, and so the science of serious archaeology can be said to have begun there. Since the year 1748, generations of skilled Italian workmen have been carefully removing the ashes that buried Pompeii, until today almost four-fifths of the city has been uncovered. Visiting Pompeii nowadays is like taking a stroll into the past—into that far-off time when the Romans ruled the world and the Emperor Titus sat on the throne of the Caesars.

Other Roman cities died more slowly. Wind and rain and fire wore them away. Later peoples tore down the ancient monuments, using the stone to build houses and churches. Over the centuries, the cities of the Caesars vanished, and all that is left of them today are scattered fragments.

Not so with Pompeii. It was engulfed in an instant, and its people's tragedy was our great gain. The buildings of Pompeii still stand as they stood 2,000 years ago, and within the houses we can still see the pots and pans, the household tools, the hammers and nails. On the walls of the buildings are election slogans and the scrawlings of unruly boys. Pompeii is like a photograph in three dimensions. It shows us exactly what a city of the Roman Empire was like, down to the smallest detail of everyday life.

To go to Pompeii today is to take a trip backward in a time machine. The old city comes to vivid life all around you. You can almost hear the clatter of horses' hoofs on the narrow streets, the cries of children, the loud hearty laughter of the shopkeepers. You can almost smell meat sizzling over a charcoal fire. The sky is cloudlessly blue, with the summer sun almost directly overhead. The grassy slopes of great Vesuvius pierce the heavens behind the city, and sunlight shimmers on the water of the bay a thousand yards from the city walls. Ships from every nation are in port, and the babble of strange languages can be heard in the streets.

Such was Pompeii on its last day. And so it is today, now that the volcanic ash has been cleared away. A good imagination is all you need to restore it to bustling vitality.

As its last day of life dawned, in A.D. 79, Pompeii found itself in the midst of a long, sleepy Mediterranean summer. It was a city several hundred years old. Its founders were an Italian people called the Oscans, who had built the city long before Rome had carved out its world-wide empire. Greeks from Naples had settled in Pompeii, too, and the walls that surrounded the city were built in the Greek style.

For more than 150 years, Pompeii had been part of the Roman Empire. The Roman dictator Sulla had besieged and captured the town in 89 B.C., giving it to his soldiers and making it a Roman colony. By A.D. 79, it had become a fashionable seaside resort, an Atlantic City or a Miami

Beach of its day. Important Romans had settled there. The great orator Cicero had been very proud of his summer home in Pompeii. It was a city of merchants and bankers, too.

Pompeii had not had unbroken peace. Twenty years earlier, in the year 59, a contest of gladiators had been held in the big outdoor stadium of Pompeii. A team of gladiators from the neighboring town of Nocera had come to fight against Pompeii's best gladiators. Tempers grew hot as local favorites were pitted against each other in combat to the death. Men from Pompeii began to hurl insults at Nocerans. Words led to blows. Then daggers flashed. A terrible massacre resulted, in which dozens of Nocerans perished and only a few escaped.

Nocera appealed to Rome, and the Roman Senate issued a stern decree: the amphitheater of Pompeii would be closed for 10 years. No more gladiatorial games! It was like having our Congress declare that neither the Yankees nor the Dodgers could play baseball for a decade.

The ruling was considered a great tragedy in sports-loving Pompeii. But an even greater one was in store four years later, in A.D. 63, for an earthquake rocked the town. Nearly every building in Pompeii toppled. Hundreds of people died.

One who survived the earthquake of 63 was the banker, Caecilius Jucundus. He was a plump, well-fed man with a harsh smile and beady eyes and a big wart on his left cheek. At the moment the earth shook, Caecilius was in the Forum, the main square of Pompeii. Much business was transacted in the Forum, which was lined with imposing stone columns arranged in a double row, one above the other.

As statues of the gods and slabs of marble tumbled to the ground, fat Caecilius sank to his knees in terror. "If my life is spared," he cried to the heavens, "I'll sacrifice a bull to the gods!"

4

We know that Caecilius escaped—and that he kept his vow. For when he rebuilt his house after the earthquake, he added a little strip of marble above his family's altar, and on it was a scene showing the earthquake and depicting the bull he had sacrificed. Next to the altar the fat money-lender kept his treasure chest, crammed full with gold coins—and, facing it, a portrait of himself, wart and all.

Sixteen years passed after the dreadful earthquake of 63. Sixteen years later, signs of the catastrophe could still be seen everywhere, for the Pompeiians were slow to rebuild. The private homes were back in order, of course, but the big public places still showed the effects of the quake. The columns of the Forum remained fallen. The Basilica, or law court, still looked devastated. The Temple of Apollo was not yet restored to its former glory. Such repairs took time and cost a great deal of money. The Pompeiians were in no hurry. Time passes slowly along the Mediterranean coast. The columns could be rebuilt next year, or the year after next, or the year after that. In time, everything would be attended to. Commerce and daily life were more important.

But time was running short.

At dawn, on the 24th of August, in the year 79, Pompeii's 25,000 people awakened to another hot day in that hot summer. There was going to be a performance in the arena that night, and the whole town was looking forward to the bloody contests of the gladiators, for the Senate's ban had long since ended. The rumble of heavy wooden wheels was heard as carts loaded with grain entered the city from the farms outside the walls. Over the centuries the steady stream of carts had worn ruts deep into the pavement of Pompeii's narrow streets.

Wooden shutters were drawn back noisily. The grocers and sellers of fruit opened their shops, displaying their wares on trays set out on the sidewalk. In the wine shops, the girls who sold wine to the thirsty sailors got ready for another busy day. Wine was the most popular drink in Pompeii—the Pompeiians drank it hot and spiced with herbs and pine resin. The wine shops were known as thermopolia. The busiest of the thermopolia belonged to Asellina, who hired pretty foreign girls to sell her wine. As the morning began, Asellina's girls waited for the first customer, and argued about politics. An election was soon to be held in Pompeii.

"Whom are you voting for?" asked Aegle the Greek, turning to Maria the Hebrew.

Maria smiled. "The same one as Zmyrina."

Zmyrina the Turk nodded. "I will vote for Caius Julius Polybius," she said, and everyone laughed. It was common knowledge around the thermopolium that Zmyrina was in love with the dashing nobleman Polybius. But Polybius was trying to pretend that Zmyrina did not exist. She had written an election slogan on the wall outside, telling people to vote for Polybius. But he did not want her support, and during the night he had covered her appeal with whitewash.

Thirsty customers crowded into Asellina's thermopolium, rowdy sailors from Africa and Greece. The political discussion ended as the girls poured the hot wine from the heavy jars. The clink of coins could be heard as the sailors put their money down, buying wine and cakes and little jars of honey.

Outside, children headed toward school, carrying slates and followed by their dogs. Nearly everyone in Pompeii had a dog, and barking could be heard everywhere as the Pompeiian pets greeted one another. A small boy who had just learned the Greek alphabet stopped in front of a blank wall and took a piece of charcoal from his tunic. Hastily he scribbled the Greek letters: *alpha, beta, gamma* . . .

In the Forum, the town's important men had gathered

6

after breakfast to read the political signs that were posted during the night. Elsewhere in the Forum, the wool merchants talked business and the men who owned the vineyards were smiling to each other about the high quality of this year's wine, which would fetch a good price in other countries.

The banker Caecilius Jucundus was going over his account books. In the Temple of Isis, the priests were preparing for the arrival of worshipers. Many of the town's richest people were spending pleasant mornings of relaxation. Quintus Poppaeus, a relative of the wife of the late Emperor Nero, was admiring his collection of fine silver treasures, made by the best craftsmen of Europe. Vesonius Primus, the rich wool merchant, had not bothered to go down to the Forum, and was passing a quiet hour in his garden. Diomedes, who had one of the largest villas in all of Pompeii, was playing with his daughter and her pet goat.

In another part of town, young Claudius Elogus, who had married only a few months before, smiled at his lovely wife. At the hotel of Sittius, late-rising travelers from the East awakened and yawned and called for breakfast. At another hotel, belonging to the politician Caius Julius Polybius, a tired merchant from Naples still slept on. He had arrived late the night before and had left orders not to be disturbed. Next door was the office of a veterinary, who was taking care of the merchant's weary horse.

The quiet morning moved slowly along. There was nothing very unusual about Pompeii. Hundreds of other towns just like it dotted the rolling plains of Italy.

But tragedy was on its way. Beneath Vesuvius' vine-covered slopes, a mighty force was about to break loose.

No one in Pompeii knew the dangerous power imprisoned in Vesuvius. For 1,500 years the mountain had slept quietly; but far beneath the crest a boiling fury of molten lava had gradually been gathering strength. The solid rock of Vesuvius held the hidden forces in check. The earthquake 16 years before had been the first sign that the trapped fury beneath the mountain was struggling to break free. Pressure was building up. In the city at the base of the mountain, life went on in complete ignorance of the looming catastrophe.

At 1 o'clock in the afternoon on the 24th of August, 79, the critical point was reached. The walls of rock could hold no longer.

The mountain exploded, raining death on thousands.

Like many tragedies, this one was misunderstood at first. Down in Pompeii, four miles from Vesuvius, a tremendous explosion was heard, echoing ringingly off the mountains on the far side of the city.

"What was that?" people cried from one end of town to another. They stared at each other, puzzled, troubled. Were the gods fighting in heaven? Is that what the loud explosion was?

"Look!" somebody shouted. "Look at Vesuvius!"

Thousands of eyes swiveled upward. Thousands of arms pointed. A black cloud was rising from the shattered crest of the mountain. Higher and higher it rose. An eyewitness, the Roman philosopher Pliny, described the cloud as he saw it from Misenum, 22 miles from Pompeii on the opposite side of the Bay:

"Better than any other tree, the pine can give an idea of the shape and appearance of this cloud," Pliny wrote in his notebook later that day. "In fact it was projected into the air like an enormous trunk and then spread into many branches, now white, now black, now spotted, according to whether earth or ashes were thrown up."

Minutes passed. The sound of the great explosion died

away, but it still tingled in everyone's ears. The cloud over Vesuvius still rose, black as night, higher and higher.

"The cloud is blotting out the sun!" someone cried in terror.

Still no one in Pompeii had perished. The fragments of rock thrown up when the mountain exploded all fell back on the volcano's slopes. Within the crater, sizzling masses of molten rock were rushing upward, and upwelling gas drove small blobs of liquefied stone thousands of feet into the air. They cooled, high above the gaping mouth of the volcano, and plummeted earthward.

A strange rain began to fall on Pompeii—a rain of stone.

The stones were light. They were pumice stones, consisting mostly of air bubbles. They poured down as though there had been a sudden cloudburst. The pumice stones, or lapilli, did little damage. They clattered against the wooden roofs of the Pompeiian houses. They fell by the hundreds in the streets. The people who had rushed out of houses and shops and thermopolia to see what had caused the explosion now scrambled to take cover as the weird rain of lapilli continued.

"What is happening?" Pompeiians asked one another. They rushed to the temples—the Temple of Jupiter, the Temple of Apollo, the Temple of Isis. Bewildered priests tried to calm bewildered citizens. Darkness had come at midday, and a rain of small stones fell from the sky, and who could explain it?

Some did not wait for explanation. In a tavern near the edge of the city, half a dozen gladiators who were scheduled to compete in that night's games decided to flee quickly. They had trumpets with them that were used to sound a fanfare at the amphitheater. But they tossed the trumpets aside, leaving them to be found centuries later. Covering their heads with tiles and pieces of wood, the gladiators rushed out into the hail of lapilli and sprinted toward the open country beyond the walls, where they hoped they would be safe.

Vesuvius was rumbling ominously, now. The sky was dark. Lapilli continued to pour down, until the streets began to clog with them.

"The eruption will be over soon!" a hopeful voice exclaimed.

But it did not end. An hour went by and darkness still shrouded everything, and still the lapilli fell. All was confusion now. Children struggled home from school, panicky in the midday darkness.

The people of Pompeii knew that doom was at hand, now. Their fears were doubled when an enormous rain of hot ashes began to fall on them, along with more lapilli. Pelted with stones, half smothered by the ashes, the Pompeiians cried out to the gods for mercy. The wooden roofs of some of the houses began to catch fire as the heat of the ashes reached them. Other buildings were collapsing under the weight of the pumice stones that had fallen on them.

In those first few hours, only the quick-witted managed to escape. Vesonius Primus, the wealthy wool merchant, called his family together and piled jewelry and money into a sack. Lighting a torch, Vesonius led his little band out into the nightmare of the streets. Overlooked in the confusion was Vesonius' black watchdog, chained in the courtyard. The terrified dog barked wildly as lapilli struck and drifting white ash settled around him. The animal struggled with his chain, battling fiercely to get free, but the chain held, and no one heard the dog's cries. The humans were too busy saving themselves.

Many hundreds of Pompeiians fled in those first few dark hours. Stumbling in the darkness, they made their way to the city gates, then out, down to the harbor. They boarded boats and got away, living to tell the tale of their city's destruction. Others preferred to remain within the city, huddling inside the temples, or in the public baths, or in the cellars of their homes. They still hoped that the nightmare would end—that the tranquillity of a few hours ago would return.

While Pompeii was being bombarded with lapilli and ash, another town near Vesuvius was meeting a different fate. Herculaneum, a town on the seashore closer to Naples, had been spared during the early hours of the eruption. Only a few lapilli had fallen there. But even while the people of Herculaneum stood watching Vesuvius and wondering what fate was befalling Pompeii, doom approached. The heat of the eruption caused water to condense on the volcano's slope. It mixed with the ashes to form a river of mud that rolled down toward Herculaneum. The mud flowed with incredible speed. It landed on Herculaneum all at once. Ten thousand people were buried within minutes, under 60 feet of mud. So rapid was the attack that no one escaped.

Neither mud nor molten lava reached Pompeii, however. Only pumice stone and ashes.

Quintus Poppaeus, the relative of Emperor Nero's wife, was one of those who decided not to abandon the city. He did not want his fine home to be looted in his absence, and he was sure that whatever had happened to Vesuvius would soon be over. Working quickly, he hid his silver treasure in the basement, 115 magnificent pieces, candlesticks and plates and silverware. Then he collected the frightened members of his family and all his servants.

"Everyone in here!" he cried, leading them to the biggest and strongest walled room of his house. "We'll be safe here! The roof will hold!"

Gathered within, they lighted a lamp and waited, silently and prayerfully, for daylight to return. But lapilli continued to thunder down on the roof. Would it hold, they wondered?

Suddenly part of the roof collapsed, blocking the door that was the only exit from the windowless room. Quintus Poppaeus barked orders to his servants: "Break a hole in the wall! We must have air!"

Someone found a pick abandoned by masons who had been repairing the room not long before. Desperately they attacked the wall, trying to chip open a passageway. Above, the roof groaned under its weight of volcanic stone.

"Hurry!" Quintus Poppaeus cried. "The roof's going to go any minute!"

By the light of the flickering lantern, the slaves worked feverishly. The hole was widened. A few of the trapped ones slipped through. Then the roof did give way, crashing down on the hapless victims caught within. They were buried under pumice, pick and lantern and all.

On the Street of Abundance, the main avenue, a Jewish sailor stepped out of a thermopolium. Shading his eyes against the fall of ash, he looked about at the destruction. He remembered a story from the Bible of how the Lord of the Hebrews had destroyed two wicked cities by sending a rain of brimstone and fire down upon them. Quickly he scrawled the names of the Biblical cities on a wall: "Sodom and Gomorrah!" Then he fled.

In his counting house, the banker Caecilius Jucundus crouched in terror. Perhaps he vowed another bull to be sacrificed if he should escape this catastrophe as he had escaped the earthquake—but this time there was to be no escape for Jucundus.

It was evening, now. And new woe was in store for Pompeii. The earth trembled and quaked! Roofs that had somehow withstood the rain of lapilli went crashing in ruin, burying hundreds who had hoped to survive the eruption. In the Forum, tall columns toppled as they had in 63. Those who remembered that great earthquake screamed in new terror as the entire city seemed to shake in the grip of a giant fist.

Three feet of lapilli now covered the ground. Ash floated in the air. Gusts of poisonous gas came drifting from the belching crater, though people could still breathe. Roofs were collapsing everywhere. The terrible cries of the dying filled the air. Rushing throngs, blinded by the darkness and the smoke, hurtled madly up one street and down the next, trampling the fallen in a crazy, fruitless dash toward safety. Dozens of people plunged into dead-end streets and found themselves trapped by crashing buildings. They waited there, too frightened to run farther, expecting the end.

The rich man Diomedes was another of those who decided not to flee at the first sign of alarm. Rather than risk being crushed by the screaming mobs, Diomedes calmly led the members of his household into the solidly built basement of his villa. Sixteen people altogether, as well as his daughter's dog and her beloved little goat. They took enough food and water to last for several days.

But for all his shrewdness and foresight, Diomedes was undone anyway. Poison gas was creeping slowly into the underground shelter! He watched his daughter begin to cough and struggle for breath. Vesuvius was giving off vast quantities of deadly carbon monoxide, that was now settling like a blanket over the dying city.

"We can't stay here!" Diomedes gasped. Better to risk the uncertainties outside than to remain here and suffocate. "I'll open the door," he told them. "Wait for me here."

Accompanied only by an old and faithful servant, who

carried a lantern to light Diomedes' way in the inky blackness, the nobleman stumbled toward the door. He held the silver key in his hand. Another few steps and he would have been at the door, he could have opened it, they could have fled into the air—but a shroud of gas swooped down on him. He fell, still clutching the key, dying within minutes. Beneath the porch, 14 people waited hopefully for him, their lives ticking away with each second. Diomedes did not return. At the last moment, all 14 embraced each other, servants and masters alike, as death took them.

The poison gas thickened as the terrible night continued. It was possible to hide from the lapilli, but not from the gas, and Pompeiians died by the hundreds. Carbon monoxide gas keeps the body from absorbing oxygen. Victims of carbon monoxide poisoning get sleepier and sleepier, until they lose consciousness, never to regain it. All over Pompeii, people lay down in the beds of lapilli, overwhelmed by the gas, and death came quietly to them. Even those who had made their way outside the city now fell victim to the spreading clouds of gas. It covered the entire countryside. Just outside one gate, on the road that led to Nocera, a giant of a man was walking rapidly away from the doomed city. Well over 6 feet tall, he carried himself with the poise and bearing of a nobleman. He was trapped by the gas and sank to the ground, his handsome face frowning as he realized that death was at hand. This aristocrat who had never knelt in his life now bent the knee to death.

At the barracks where the gladiators lived, men whose business it was to face death for other men's amusement now saw the end coming for all. They shook their fists at the sky and shouted curses at the gods. A rich woman, bedecked with jewels, rushed into the barracks. She was terrified of the wild mobs outside.

"Protect me!" she cried.

But the gladiators, strong men that they were, could protect no one, not even themselves. And as the gas seeped into their room, they died, the rich woman among them.

Two prisoners, left behind in the jail when their keepers fled, pounded on the sturdy wooden doors. "Let us out!" they called. But no one heard, and the gas entered. They died, not knowing that the jailers outside were dying as well.

In a lane near the Forum, a hundred people were trapped by a blind-alley wall. Others hid in the stoutly built public bathhouses, protected against collapsing roofs but not against the deadly gas. Near the house of Diomedes, a beggar and his little goat sought shelter. The man fell dead a few feet from Diomedes' door; the faithful goat remained by his side, its silver bell tinkling, until its turn came.

All through the endless night, Pompeiians wandered about the streets or crouched in their ruined homes or clustered in the temples to pray. By morning, few remained alive. Not once had Vesuvius stopped hurling lapilli and ash into the air, and the streets of Pompeii were filling quickly. At midday on August 25, exactly 24 hours after the beginning of the holocaust, a second eruption racked the volcano. A second cloud of ashes rose above Vesuvius' summit. The wind blew ash as far as Rome and Egypt. But most of the new ashes descended on Pompeii.

The deadly shower of stone and ashes went unslackening into its second day. But it no longer mattered to Pompeii whether the eruption continued another day or another year. For by midday on August 25, Pompeii was a city of the dead.

It is possible to reconstruct the happenings during the last days of Pompeii, names and all, because of the city's unique preservation throughout the centuries—and because of the care that has gone into its rediscovery. Pompeii was buried in one great holocaust, and the suddenness of the cataclysm left records untouched, houses nearly intact, and even small household articles unharmed. Contrary to popular belief, Pompeii was not crushed under lava, nor did it burn. It was smothered by pumice stone and poison gas. Consequently relatively little damage was done when the end came.

The first excavators of Pompeii were the fortunate few survivors, who returned some days after the eruption had ceased. They found their city buried beneath an enormous mass of volcanic ash. No sign of life was anywhere. Mourning for their lost relatives and friends, they ventured out onto the warm covering of the city and dug downward to reach their homes. They brought out what they could find of their property. But this kind of digging was risky and difficult; they soon abandoned hope of salvaging much, and left the buried city.

A year after the eruption, Emperor Titus stopped off at Vesuvius to inspect the zone of destruction. By that time only the tops of the highest towers were visible. Drifting ash had hidden all the rest. Titus, the conqueror of Jerusalem, noted how the gods could destroy at will, and left the site.

The years passed. Pompeii and Herculaneum became vague memories, and then not even that. The Roman Empire reached the zenith of its power under Trajan and Hadrian, and then began the long, slow decline into darkness. Centuries came and went, and grass grew over the sites of the buried cities ringing Vesuvius.

In the sixteenth century an Italian nobleman, Count Sarno-Muzio-Tuttavilla, ordered that a canal be dug underground to bring the water of the Sarno River to the town of Torre Annunziata, near Vesuvius. In the course of the excavation, the workmen came across some ruins which the count believed were those of Stabia, a seacoast town destroyed by the dictator Sulla in 89 B.C. Actually, the count's workmen had rediscovered forgotten Pompeii. But they did not realize this, and no further excavations were made.

The next time the ruins were disturbed was in 1709. An Austrian prince named D'Elboeuf, having a well dug in the woods not far from Vesuvius, came upon the walls of a theater. The ruins were buried under 50 feet of rock-hard lava and mud.

D'Elboeuf realized the importance of his find. It was Herculaneum, whose sudden end had been recorded by eyewitnesses centuries earlier. It was ironic that Herculaneum should have been excavated before Pompeii, since the task of exploring Herculaneum was far more difficult.

For seven years D'Elboeuf sunk shafts into the solidified mud over Herculaneum. As though mining coal, his workmen hacked horizontal galleries through the lava deep below the surface of the earth, and carved their way into the streets and houses of the buried town. There was no such thing as archaeological technique then, and D'Elboeuf's workmen smashed their way crudely into the buildings, doing grave damage. They brought up statues and marbles of great beauty. This was not archaeology but simple robbery; D'Elboeuf's finds were carried off to ornament the homes of the nobility, and no attempt was made to study them in any serious manner.

In 1738, Charles of Bourbon, King of the Two Sicilies, took as his wife Maria Amalia Christine, daughter of the Elector of Saxony. The royal couple settled in Naples, where many of D'Elboeuf's finds had been brought as decorations for the palace of the Bourbon kings. The young queen, delighted by the beauty of the statuary, expressed

17

interest in the old excavations and urged her husband to organize a new expedition to explore buried Herculaneum.

The king agreed. Vesuvius had burst into life again in May, 1737, but had been quiet since then. Excavations were renewed at D'Elboeuf's old site on the side of the volcano. A Spanish engineer, Cavaliere Rocco Gioacchino de Alcubierre, was placed in charge of the operation. Following D'Elboeuf's old shafts, his men probed downward until the ring of metal against metal told them that their picks were striking statues. Huge bronze figures of men on horseback were found and brought to the surface.

For the first time an expert now entered the picture. He was the Marchese Don Marcello Venuti, keeper of the royal library. He supervised the excavations and prevented any further wanton damage from being done. Entering the shafts, he translated inscriptions and positively identified the subterranean ruins as those of Herculaneum. Old records now were examined and it was learned that another city, Pompeii, was somewhere nearby—buried not under all-but-impassable rock, but rather under light and easily removed pumice.

But the actual site of the other city eluded the diggers for more than a decade. The discovery of Pompeii was accidental, again made by canal diggers. On April 1, 1748, excavations began at Pompeii. Within five days, a great pit had been opened and much of the pumice was removed. A magnificent wall painting was discovered. Two weeks later, a skeleton was found, surrounded by gold and silver coins that had rolled from the dying man's desperate grasp.

The things that came from the pit at Pompeii were only of minor interest to the royal excavator. King Charles appreciated the marble statues, the gold and silver objects, the paintings and elegant mosaics. But he had no interest in the ordinary daily things, the wine jars and dishes and cooking utensils. He was no scholar—simply an educated dilettante with a love for beautiful things. Therefore, every time the flow of treasure began to peter out, the king ordered the excavation shifted to another part of the site.

The work was thus slipshod and disorderly. To add to the confusion, 12 of Alcubierre's 24 workmen were criminals forced to dig as punishment for their crimes. These coarse and resentful men hardly bothered to take much pains in their digging. It was easier to smash through a wall than to unearth it carefully, and what did they care if they ruined a priceless painting on the other side? They were quick to steal, too, and many small gold and silver objects found their way into the workmen's pockets and thence to dealers on the outside, who had them melted down for their value as metal alone.

Still, excavations continued, both at Pompeii and at the vastly more difficult site of Herculaneum. The palace of the Bourbons began to fill with recovered treasure—objects which can be seen today in the Museo Nazionale at Naples. Digging at random, the excavators opened pit after pit, filling them in when the stream of gold and silver dried up.

Work continued on this hit-or-miss basis for some years. Even though this was the richest treasure-trove of man's past that had then come to light, King Charles permitted few scholars to study the finds. A man named Bayardi was allowed to compile a catalogue of the Pompeii-Herculaneum discoveries, but he seems to have been more of a courtier and politician than a true archaeologist. By 1752, he had turned out five volumes of worthless commentary on the recovered treasures, while at the same time busily scheming to prevent legitimate students of antiquity from visiting the site.

At length the famous Johann Joachim Winckelmann entered the picture. Winckelmann, considered the founder of modern scientific archaeology, was the son of a cobbler, born in Prussia in 1717. His love of the past sent him all over the Prussian countryside as a boy, poking into caves and tunnels in search of ancient relics. At the age of 31 Winckelmann left Prussia for Saxony, where, as librarian for the Count of Bünau, near Dresden, he had access to a fine collection of Greek and Roman antiquities.

Winckelmann resolved to go to Italy, where the relics of Imperial Rome could be studied first hand. To smooth his way, he became a Catholic, even though he was not a man of strong religious feelings. Settling in Rome, Winckelmann heard of the remarkable discoveries being made in the vicinity of Vesuvius, and sought permission to explore the site.

But Italy in the eighteenth century was not a unified nation. Naples and the surrounding area were ruled by the King of the Two Sicilies; Rome was governed by the Pope. Winckelmann ran into difficulties when he tried to view the excavations or even the collection at the Royal Museum in Naples. He wangled permission to visit the Museum, finally, but he was treated like a spy from an enemy country. He was closely watched and not allowed to make a sketch of any object whatsoever.

By a combination of perseverance, courage, and bribery, Winckelmann managed to get to see the excavations, and in 1762 published his first study on the subject, *On the Discoveries at Herculaneum*. In the same year he was appointed Chief Supervisor of all antiquities in and about Rome, and with this title he was able to obtain a closer look at the Pompeii-Herculaneum diggings. He published a second commentary in 1764, and also his important book, *History of the Art of Antiquity*, which attempted to classify and analyze the entire body of objects recovered from the ruins of the ancient world.

Many of Winckelmann's theories about Greece and Rome have proved to be false as further excavations clarified what was then an extremely hazy record. But his importance as a pioneer cannot be ignored. Before Winckelmann, it was considered ungentlemanly to dig for evidence. Hypotheses about the ancient lands were conceived in ivory towers by dreamy-eyed scholars. Winckelmann believed in going to the sites—digging—looking. He established a systematic practice for archaeological research that had not existed before him. And his work rescued Pompeii and Herculaneum from the amateurs and the dilettantes who had been ruining the scientific value of the sites in their quest for pretty statuettes.

Winckelmann died in 1768, murdered by an Italian criminal in a wayside inn. But the work at Pompeii and Herculaneum continued. Changing political conditions caused the abandonment of excavation for long periods of time, and what work was done before 1860 was concerned largely with uncovering the important buildings—the theaters, the large houses, and the Forum.

In 1860, the Bourbon Kings of the Two Sicilies were driven into exile by the forces of Garibaldi, one of the men chiefly responsible for the unification of Italy into a single country. The unification took place the following year when the Pope was forced to give up political control of the area around Rome. The new government inaugurated an ambitious plan of excavating the treasures of the past, and under this scheme work began once again at Pompeii. (Herculaneum was considered too difficult to uncover, and serious digging did not begin there until 1927.)

The new director of the Pompeii project was Giuseppe

21

Fiorelli. He rejected the idea of digging at random, as had been done before, and instead directed his men to move through the city street by street, fully uncovering one area before going on to another. In this way—and under careful archaeological supervision—Pompeii began to emerge finally from its shroud of pumice and ash.

Fiorelli also hit on an unusual idea that has greatly aided in visualizing the tragedy of Pompeii. Ashes had piled up around many perishable objects and had hardened into molds over the centuries. The objects themselves had long since turned to powder, but holes in the ashes remained, in the exact shapes of the original artifacts.

With infinite care Fiorelli had his men pour liquid plaster into these hollow molds. The result was a cast with the precise form of the model. In this way, casts of staircases, cart wheels, articles of furniture, and other wooden implements were made and are now on exhibition in a small museum at Pompeii. And not only furniture was preserved by this method. Pompeiians themselves, trapped by the ashes, left molds that Fiorelli used. And so we have not only skeletons, but plaster casts of the victims themselves, some of them calm and relaxed as the end approached, others horribly twisted, their faces contorted with fear. In this way it was possible to reconstruct the last day exactly, down to facial expressions and the positions of the fallen dead. Even dogs and goats have been modeled in this way. The casts have been called "snapshots taken by a magic camera." Fiorelli's brilliant idea has brought us the Pompeiians almost in the flesh, preserved in their clothing and shoes, in the moment of their doom.

Since Fiorelli's time the excavations have gone on steadily. Generations of Italian workmen have labored on the site, bringing away pound after pound of ash and pumice. Uncovering the ancient city is virtually a sacred trust today, son following father at the work. More than 600,000 cubic meters of earth have been taken from the diggings and deposited in the marshes along the nearby Sarno River. Within the next few years, probably, the last of Pompeii's 165,000 acres will have been cleared, and the entire city will stand visible.

Work at Herculaneum is progressing, too, though far more slowly because of the more difficult nature of the problem. Other, smaller Roman villages are still believed to remain buried, and so excavations in the Vesuvius area will continue for a long time to come.

Although two centuries ago poor Winckelmann had to bribe his way to see Pompeii, today it is visited freely by thousands of tourists each year. A fine modern superhighway leads from Naples to Pompeii, and friendly guides speaking many languages are employed by the Italian Government to help visitors experience anew the tragedy of Pompeii.

Arriving at Pompeii today, you leave your car outside and enter through an age-old gate. Just within the entrance is a museum that has been built in recent years to house many of the smaller antiquities found in the ruins. Here are statuettes and toys, saucepans and loaves of bread. The account books of the banker Caecilius Jucundus are there, noting all the money he had lent at steep interest rates. Glass cups, coins, charred beans and peas and turnips, baskets of grapes and plums and figs, a box of chestnuts—the little things of Pompeii have all been miraculously preserved for your startled eyes.

Then you enter the city proper. The streets are narrow and deeply rutted with the tracks of chariot wheels. Only special narrow Pompeiian chariots could travel inside the town. Travelers from outside were obliged to change vehicles when they reached the walls of the city. This provided a profitable monopoly for the Pompeiian equivalent of cab drivers, 20 centuries ago!

At each intersection, blocks of stone several feet high are mounted in the roadway, so designed that chariot wheels could pass on either side of them.

"Those are steppingstones for the people of Pompeii," your guide tells you. "Pompeii had no sewers, and during heavy rainfalls the streets were flooded with many inches of water. The Pompeiians could keep their feet dry by walking on those stones."

Streets stretch straight ahead of you. The city is roughly oval in shape, and the streets are very carefully laid out, crossing each other at right angles everywhere but in a few isolated corners of the city, which must have been older than the rest. In this respect it is a little like Manhattan island, which is laid out with mathematical precision except at the southern tip that was settled in the seventeenth century, a crazy quilt of irregular, twisting streets.

But Pompeii's streets, though straight, are certainly narrow. The widest is only 32 feet across; most of the main avenues are only 20 feet wide, and the side streets are mere alleyways, no more than 14 feet in width.

The houses and shops are of stone. The upper stories, which were wooden, were burned away in the holocaust or simply crumbled with the centuries. The biggest of the shops are along the Street of Abundance, which must have been the Fifth Avenue of its day. Silversmiths, shoemakers, manufacturers of cloth—all had their shops here. And every few doors, there is another thermopolium, or wine shop. In many of these, the big jars of wine are still intact, standing in holes in marble counters just the way bins of ice cream are stored in a soda fountain today.

At the center of the city, the Street of Abundance is crossed at right angles by the other main street, the Stabian

24

Way, and at this intersection are located the Stabian Baths, the oldest of Pompeii's public bathhouses. At the baths, the bathers had their choice of hot, cool, or lukewarm water. Big pools were maintained at different temperatures. Although a relatively small city, Pompeii boasted three baths. The second was at the Forum, and the third, under construction at another important intersection, would have been bigger than either of the other two had it been finished before the cataclysm.

Against a hillside is the theatrical district of the city—two theaters, a large and a small, in a triangular area looking down on the Sarno River. Nearby is the barracks where the gladiators lived. The big theater could seat about 5,000 spectators, but it was completely open to the elements. The smaller theater, seating 1,500, had a permanent roof.

Pompeii also had an amphitheater where the gladiatorial contests were held. It could seat about 20,000, or nearly the entire population of the city. No doubt people came from the neighboring towns to witness the gladiatorial contests held at Pompeii.

The center of the city's life was the Forum, a large square which you enter not far from the main gate of the city. Before the earthquake of 63, Pompeii's Forum must have been a truly imposing place, enclosed on three sides by a series of porticoes supported by huge columns. At the north end, on the fourth side, stood the temple of Jupiter, Juno, and Minerva, raised on a podium 10 feet high. But the earthquake toppled the temple and most of the columns, and not much rebuilding had been done at the time of the eruption. Pompeii's slowness to rebuild was our eternal loss, for little remains of the Forum except the stumps of massive columns.

The Forum in its heyday was closed to vehicles. Men on foot entered and transacted their business there. On the south side stood the halls of the city's officials; on the east was the hall of the Comitium, where elections were held each year. On the west side were located the temple of Apollo, the city treasury, the bureau of weights and measures, and the basilica, or law court, which before the earthquake had a towering roof and three huge naves or aisles.

Other public buildings were also on the main square: the headquarters of the wool industry, and several other temples, including one dedicated to Vespasian (father of Titus), a Roman emperor who was worshiped as a deity. Near the Forum was a macellum, or market, where foodstuffs were sold and where beggars wandered.

Pompeii had many beggars. One of them was found in April, 1957, at the gate of the road leading to the town of Nocera. A cast taken of him shows him to have been less than 5 feet tall, and deformed by the bone disease known as rickets. On the last day of Pompeii's life, this beggar had gone about asking for alms, and some generous citizen had given him a bone with a piece of meat still adhering to it. When the eruption came, the beggar tried to flee, jealously guarding his precious sack containing the cutlet—and he was found with it, 2,000 years later.

Pompeii was a city of many fine temples, both around the Forum and in the outlying streets. One of the most interesting is one dating from the sixth century B.C., the oldest building in the city. Only the foundation and a few fragmented columns remain, but this temple was evidently regarded with great reverence, since it was located in the center of a fairly large triangular space adjoining the main theater. Nearby is the Temple of Isis, which was rebuilt after the earthquake and so is in fairly good preservation. Isis, an Egyptian goddess, was one of the many foreign gods and goddesses who had come to be worshiped in the Roman Empire by the time of the destruction of Pompeii. Her gaudily decorated temple at Pompeii is the only European temple of Isis that has come down to us from the ancient world.

But many temples, bathhouses, amphitheaters, and government buildings have survived in other places. What makes Pompeii uniquely significant is the wealth of knowledge it gives us about the *private* lives of its people. Nowhere else do we have such complete information about the homes of the ancients, about their customs and living habits, about their humble pots and pans.

The houses in Pompeii show the evolution of styles over a period of several centuries. Many of the houses are built to the same simple plan: a central court, known as the atrium, around which a living room, bedrooms, and a garden are arrayed. This was the classic Roman style of home. Some of the later and more impressive houses show the influence of Greek styles, with paintings and mosaic decorations as well as baths, reception rooms, huge gardens, and sometimes a second atrium.

The houses of Pompeii are known by name, and a good deal is known of their occupants. One of the most famous is the House of the Vetti Brothers, which is lavishly decorated with paintings, mosaics, and sculptures. The inscriptions on these houses are often amusing today. One businessman had written on the walls of his villa, WELCOME PROFITS! Another greeted his visitors with the inscribed words, PROFITS MEAN JOY!

At the so-called House of the Tragic Poet, a mosaic shows a barking dog, with the inscription *cave canem*— "Beware of the dog." On the building known as the House of the Lovers, which received its name because the newly married Claudius Elogus lived there, someone had written

27

a line of verse dedicated to the newlyweds on the porch: *Amantes, ut apes, vitam mellitem exigunt.* ("Lovers, like bees, desire a life full of honey.")

The House of the Gilt Cupids had a garden filled with statuettes and a fishpond in the courtyard. The House of Menander, which belonged to Quintus Poppaeus, had recently been redecorated, and its wall paintings are particularly fine. (The house is known as the House of Menander because Quintus Poppaeus, a lover of the theater, had had a portrait of the Greek comic playwright Menander placed on one of the walls.)

One interesting house uncovered since World War II is the Villa of Giulia Felix ("Happy Julia") which was of exceptional size. Apparently Giulia found the expense of this elegant house too much for her budget, because she had opened her baths to the public and advertised the fact with a sign on the gate. For a fee, Pompeiians who scorned the crowds at the public baths could bathe at Giulia's in privacy and comfort. Even this income does not seem to have been enough, for another sign uncovered in 1953 announced that the magnificent villa was for rent.

When you visit Pompeii, you go from one splendid house to the next. The guide tells you, "This was the house of Diomedes," or "This was the house of Vesonius," and if you stand in the courtyard and exercise your imagination you can almost begin to see the rich Pompeiians stepping out of the shadows. Because of the skeletal findings, we know how these important people met their doom, and some of their stories were told in the first part of this chapter.

One of the truly fascinating aspects of Pompeii is the multitude of scribbled street signs. Notices were painted directly on the stone, and have come down to us. At the big amphitheater, an inscription tells us, "The troupe of gladiators owned by Suettius Centus will give a performance at Pompeii on May 31st. There will be an animal show. The awnings will be used." And at the theater where plays were given, a message to a popular actor reads, "Actius, beloved of the people, come back soon; fare thee well!"

There are inscriptions at the taverns, too. "Romula loves Staphyclus" is on one wall. Elsewhere there is a poem that sounds like one of today's hit tunes: "Anyone could as well stop the winds blowing, / And the waters from flowing, / As stop lovers from loving."

Some Pompeiians scribbled proverbs, such as, "A little evil grows great if disregarded." Another man, with a sly sense of humor, left this: "Everyone writes on the walls— except me." At another tavern, some jovial soul wrote, "Greetings! We are most valiant drinking men! When you came, we paid the bill!" And another says, "Curse you, landlord! You sell water for wine and drink unmixed wine yourself!"

Election notices were posted everywhere. One says, "Siccia demands that Trebius and Gavius be elected aediles." Another mentions a candidate and says, "The wool merchants want him to be elected." Other announcements were not so polite. Pompeiians were often coarse and vulgar in their wall inscriptions, and some are completely unprintable.

Wherever you turn in Pompeii, echoes of the dead city strike you. In one rich house, a breakfast set in silver, complete with two egg cups, was found. Shopping lists were discovered. Wall paintings show religious ceremonies, games, and everyday amusements. The vats used for bleaching cloth for togas still remain. In some of the 20 bakeries, newly baked loaves stand on the counters.

To enter Pompeii is to step into the Rome of the Caesars. An entire city, forever frozen in the last moment of its life by a terrible cataclysm, awaits the visitor. Thanks to the painstaking work of generations of devoted Italian archaeologists, we can experience today the most minute details of life 20 centuries ago in a Roman city. So much do we know of the people of Pompeii that they take on vivid life for us—the banker Jucundus, the wool merchant Vesonius, the newlywed Claudius Elogus, the nobleman Diomedes. The dreadful eruption that snatched the life of these people and this city in a single day also gave it a kind of immortality. Pompeii and its people live on today, in timeless permanence, their city transformed by Vesuvius' fury into a miraculous survivor of the ancient world.

2 | Homer's Troy

The *Iliad* of Homer is the first and perhaps the greatest war story ever told. It is the story of how Paris, the light-hearted son of Priam, King of Troy, stole the wife of Menelaus, King of Sparta. Menelaus' wife was Helen, the loveliest woman in the world.

Homer sings of the revenge against Troy. Menelaus' brother Agamemnon, King of Mycenae and the chief ruler of Greece, leads a mighty host against offending Troy when Paris mockingly refuses to return the stolen Helen. All the kings of Greece assemble: valiant Achilles, wily Odysseus, mighty Ajax, aged Nestor, and the rest. An enormous army camps on the Trojan plain. But Troy, led by Paris' warrior brother Hector, stands off the Greeks for nine years. The besiegers begin to quarrel among themselves, great Achilles withdrawing to sulk in his tents when he feels he has been insulted by Agamemnon.

But then the gods themselves intervene in the stalemated conflict. The plot tightens: Achilles leaves his tent and slays doughty Hector; the *Iliad* ends with the scene of Hector's funeral. In the *Odyssey*, Homer tells us of how, through a ruse of clever Odysseus, the walls of Troy were

31

breached and the city destroyed, and of the decade-long homeward wandering of Odysseus afterward.

These two great stories have glowed with life for thousands of years and still exert their old magic. The anger of Achilles, the homeward journey of Odysseus—these are unforgettable stories, enduring epics that will survive eternally.

But is there any historic basis to them? Gods and goddesses, fantastic creatures and mysterious giants, these are the trappings of fantasy—but was there such a war, such a place as Troy, such kings as Priam and Agamemnon? For centuries no one knew. Homer's poems were considered to be marvelous stories, the greatest ever told, but there was no way of knowing what historical actualities underlay the myths and the fantasy. As late as 1846, George Grote's *History of Greece* remarked: "Though literally believed, reverentially cherished, and numbered among the gigantic phenomena of the past, by the Grecian public, it [the Trojan War] is in the eyes of modern enquiry essentially a legend and nothing more. If we are asked whether it be not a legend embodying portions of historical matter, and raised upon a basis of truth . . . if we are asked whether there was not really some such historical Trojan war as this, our answer must be, that as the possibility of it cannot be denied, so neither can the reality of it be affirmed. We possess nothing but the ancient epic itself without any independent evidence."

But the evidence existed—buried in the ground. And, even as Grote's book appeared, a young man of 24 dreamed of finding Priam's Troy, Homer's Troy, and proving forever that the great poems of Homer were based on historical happenings.

He was Heinrich Schliemann, born in 1822 in the little village of Ankershagen, Germany. His father was a poor but well-educated clergyman, who amused young Heinrich by telling him stories of ancient Troy, tales of Hector and Achilles, Agamemnon and Priam. Heinrich heard these stories over and over again until they became part of him. He retold them to his playmates. In his imagination, he stood with Achilles outside the walls of Troy; he relived with Odysseus the 10-year journey home to Ithaca.

When the boy was 7, in 1829, his father gave him as a Christmas present a copy of Jerrer's *Universal History of the World*. The serious-minded boy turned the pages of the massive volume, poring over the pages of closely printed text.

Suddenly he came to an illustration that brought him up with a startled cry. It showed Aeneas, one of the Trojan heroes, escaping from the blazing city. Flames danced along the walls and around the great Scaean Gate.

"Father!" Heinrich cried. "You told me that Troy was all gone, that it had vanished from the earth!"

"So it has," the father replied.

"There is nothing left?"

"Nothing, Heinrich."

"But look, look here," the boy persisted. "Here is a picture of Troy in flames! How could the man have drawn such a picture if Troy no longer exists?"

The father chuckled. "That is only a fanciful picture, Heinrich. It was not drawn from the real city of Troy."

"But did Troy have huge walls like these in the picture?"

"Yes, I suppose it did."

"Then they must exist!" Heinrich declared triumphantly. "Such great walls could not disappear completely! They must be hidden somewhere under the ground. And *I* shall dig them up!"

The elder Schliemann must have smiled indulgently at that conversation. But Heinrich was serious, even at the age of 7. Troy, he knew, *had* to have survived the ages. Those mighty walls had held off the Greeks for nearly 10 years and could not have crumbled completely into ruin. And some day he would find them—would find the Troy of which Homer sang.

Heinrich Schliemann grew up obsessed with Troy and with Homer. When a drunken miller's helper began to recite the *Iliad* in Greek, Schliemann paid him to recite the passages a second time, even though he understood not a word. Simply hearing the actual words of Homer was a thrill for him. He told a girl he loved, when he was 14, that some day he would discover lost Troy. The dream never lost its power over him.

When he was 19, he went to sea. Shipwrecked off the Netherlands, he settled in Amsterdam and found a job as an office boy. Living alone in a single tiny room, he began to study languages, teaching himself English, French, Dutch, Spanish, Portuguese, and Italian within two years. His fluency brought him promotions, and by the age of 22 he had become correspondent and bookkeeper of an Amsterdam firm doing business with Russia. Of course, he taught himself Russian as well, and within six weeks could speak it fluently.

His firm sent him to Russia in 1846. This experience helped him to found his own export-import firm, and soon he was a prosperous businessman. He traveled widely, amassed a fortune by the time he was 30, made an unhappy marriage, and continued to add to his amazing collection of languages. By the time he was 33 he was fluent in 15 languages, including Polish, Swedish, Norwegian, Slovenian, Danish, Latin, and both modern and ancient Greek. Oddly, he saved ancient Greek—the language of Homer—for last. The needs of commerce came first. But finally he could read the story of Troy in the original.

His astonishing career reads like something from a story-book. In 1850 he visited the United States to settle the financial affairs of his brother Louis, who had gone to America and died there of typhus. While Schliemann was in California, the gold rush broke out, and almost accidentally he made another fortune. He also became an American citizen.

Eight years later, Schliemann made his first trip through the Middle East, from Cairo to Jerusalem. Quite naturally, he learned Arabic while journeying. Then it was back to Europe for business affairs. Incredibly wealthy now, he began to think of retiring from commerce and devoting his time to archaeological studies—in particular, to the location of the city of Troy.

Most scholars of Schliemann's time believed that the stories of Homer were pure myth. There were a few who stubbornly clung to the notion that there really had been a Troy, but most scholars were of the opinion that all the fine descriptions were simply products of Homer's splendid imagination. The scoffers offered substantial reasons for this belief. When the Greeks had made their first recorded appearance in history, they had been a small and simple people. They did not have great fleets of mighty ships, or huge cities, or towering palaces. Yet Homer had depicted a society of much earlier times as one that boasted a thousand ships and splendid palaces and cities. Had all the majesty of Homeric Greece been swallowed up by Time? It was simpler to believe that Homer had been inventing than to think that Greece had once been great, had lapsed back into darkness for hundreds of years, and then once again had attained power and glory. Agamemnon and the rest were pure legends, these skeptics said.

But Schliemann refused to hear them. He had all the evidence he needed. Homer's descriptions of shields and ships and chariots were too accurate to be mere works of imagination. No one, Schliemann insisted, could have visualized a mythical society in such vivid detail. Troy was real! It *had* to be!

Now a millionaire several times over, and 46 years old, Schliemann set out in 1868 to find Troy. His old dream had never faded, and now he had the wealth to underwrite an expedition.

In 1868 he went to Greece, visiting Ithaca, the city of Odysseus. He wrote, "I forgot heat and thirst. . . . Now I was investigating the neighborhood, reading in the *Odyssey* the stirring scenes enacted there, now admiring the splendid panorama." He told of sitting in the village square and reading Homer to the descendants of fabled Odysseus, who wept as he read the verses.

He did some archaeological research, too. He dug at a mound called "The Castle of Odysseus" by the Ithacans, and recovered urns containing human ashes, a sacrificial knife, and a few clay idols. Schliemann persuaded himself that he had actually found the tomb of Odysseus.

But finding Troy was much more important. He visited Mycenae, the city of Agamemnon, and then crossed the Dardanelles strait into Asia Minor. The traditional location of Troy was there, on the coast of Asian Turkey. He roamed the countryside, wondering whether perhaps Troy lay directly beneath his feet.

But he needed companionship—a woman's love—before he could truly begin his quest. His marriage had been unsuccessful, and he now took the step of going to America, where divorces were more easily obtained, in order to divorce his wife. At the same time he wrote to a Greek friend, a priest named Vimpos, who had now become the Archbishop of Athens, and asked him to "choose for me a wife of the same angelic character as your married sister.

She should be poor, but well educated; she must be enthusiastic about Homer and about the rebirth of my beloved Greece. . . . She should be of the Greek type, with black hair, and, if possible, beautiful. But my main requirement is a good and loving heart."

The archbishop found a girl to fit all of Schliemann's requirements. She was just sixteen, a beautiful Greek lass named Sophia. Loving, attractive, and skilled in history and poetry, she was all Schliemann could have wanted, and she was willing to marry him. The 47-year-old Schliemann took Sophia as his wife in 1869, and together they set out to find Troy.

If Troy had existed at all, the scholars felt, its site was probably a village called Bunarbashi on the coast of Asia Minor. The sole reason for selecting Bunarbashi as the site was a passage in the 22nd Book of the *Iliad,* which said that near Troy there were two springs: "In one of these the water comes up hot; steam rises from it and hangs about like smoke above a blazing fire. But the other, even in summer, gushes up as cold as hail or freezing snow or water that has turned to ice."

There were two such springs at Bunarbashi. The difference in temperature between them was not very great, only a few degrees, but there *was* a difference—and nowhere else in the area were there two springs of different temperatures. Also, Bunarbashi stood at the southern end of the plain known as the Plain of Troy, with rocky heights behind it that would make it an ideal place for a citadel.

But Schliemann scorned the idea that the muddy village of Bunarbashi could be the site of Troy. It was eight miles from the coast, for one thing, and the *Iliad* told of the Greeks going back and forth from their ships to Troy several times on the same day. The true Troy, Schliemann reasoned, could be no more than three miles or so from the coast. And Achilles had chased Hector three times around the walls of Troy before killing him—which could not have been done at Bunarbashi because of its location, Schliemann argued. The clincher came when he tested the springs, the famous springs of Bunarbashi. He found not two but 34, and all of them cold.

No, Bunarbashi could not be the site of Troy, whatever the scholars maintained. Schliemann moved his camp elsewhere.

His new location was the village of Hissarlik, an hour's distance from the coast. After a quick preliminary survey, Schliemann nodded in satisfaction. "This is the site of Troy," he announced in tones that left no room for doubt. "Here we will dig, and here we will find Troy!"

It seems presumptuous for Schliemann to have jumped so quickly to such a sweeping conclusion. But Schliemann had always been one to listen to the inner voice rather than to what others told him, and he had rarely been wrong. Now the inner voice told him that Hissarlik was Troy.

The evidence was fairly impressive. Hissarlik's very name meant "Palace." In historic times, the Romans had built a settlement here atop an earlier Greek town, and the settlement had been known as Novum Ilium—New Troy. Ruins of New Troy still could be found. Legend had it that New Troy had been built on the site of Priam's Troy.

The spot had had importance in the past. The Persian King Xerxes had sacrificed a thousand oxen at Novum Ilium. Alexander the Great had offered sacrifices at the temple there. Surely they had come because this was the site of Troy!

The geography bore Schliemann out. There were no springs at all, but geologists assured him that it was by no

38

means unusual for springs to dry out over a span of some 3,000 years. And the location of Hissarlik was perfect. Schliemann wrote: "One is astonished to see that this noble mound of Hissarlik seems to have been intended by Nature herself to be the site of a great citadel. If well fortified, the location would command the whole plain of Troy. In the whole region there is no point comparable with this one."

The mound rose 162 feet. The ruins of an ancient city were clearly apparent just beneath the surface. In fact, it seemed as though city upon city upon city had been built there, with the Turks just the latest of many. The hill sloped gently, making possible a battle such as that between Hector and Achilles. To circle the city three times at Hissarlik, the two warriors would have had to run nine miles—not impossible, Schliemann thought. At Bunarbashi they could not have run around the city at all, so steep is the drop at several places.

This was the place, Schliemann decided, and nothing could shake his opinion.

In April, 1870, he began to dig.

The first excavations turned up the ruined Roman city of Novum Ilium, which had been built perhaps in the second or third century B.C. Obviously, many other cities lay below. Schliemann abandoned the digging for a while to replan his attack, then resumed in September of 1871. He led 80 workmen in the assault on Hissarlik.

Soon he was jubilant with excitement. He got below the Roman level and found, so he claimed, the walls of Troy. He wrote: "I have discovered the ruins of palaces and temples on walls of much older buildings, and at the depth of fifteen feet I came upon huge walls six feet thick and of most wonderful construction. Seven and a half feet lower down I found that these walls rested upon other walls eight and a half feet thick. These must be the walls of the palace of Priam or the temple of Minerva."

The scholarly world regarded Schliemann as a fool and a charlatan. So he had found walls! Who said they were the walls of Troy? What did he know about archaeology? He was nothing but a rich businessman—an amateur. Why believe that these particular walls were the walls of Priam?

To his own embarrassment, Schliemann soon discovered that he had been too quick to form his judgment. If the walls he had found were the walls of Priam's city, what was all this that lay beneath? There were still other cities below, in this fantastic archaeological sandwich. Which, if any, was the real Troy?

He did not know. He kept digging.

The scholars were right in one respect. Schliemann *was* an amateur, and he committed all the amateur's sins in archaeology, at least at the outset. A trained archaeologist approaches a site with the delicacy of a surgeon performing a risky operation. Each layer of soil is peeled back with minute care, and the camel's-hair brush and the tweezers are used as often as the pickax. The idea is to uncover each layer cautiously and to identify everything thoroughly before continuing deeper.

But Schliemann, bubbling over with the desire to unearth Troy, and untrained in scientific archaeological methods, went smashing down through layer after layer with ruthless abandon. He was not interested in the clutter of later cities that overlay his precious Troy. He hacked his way down through them, demolishing and destroying without bothering to photograph and record. He cut a great trench straight down into the hill, ripping away anything that seemed unimportant to his main quest. Only later, when he had taken on a professional archaeologist as his assistant, was he more careful with the higher strata.

With Sophia at his side, Schliemann dug deeper and deeper into the puzzle box of piled-up cities. From September to November, 1871, Schliemann's workers drove a trench 33 feet below the surface of the hill on the northern slope. Winter forced him to retreat, but he returned again in March, 1872, this time with 150 workmen and the best equipment available, along with three overseers and an engineer. He had a four-room house built atop Hissarlik to use as headquarters.

Down, down, down. Mosquitoes and fevers plagued him. The water was bad. The workers were stubborn, lazy, and destructive. The Turkish authorities, perturbed by the size of the hole he was digging, harried and chivied him.

Still the hole went down. He worked in the trench alongside his men, except when he came down with malaria. At night, Sophia would sort through the day's finds: fragments of pottery, idols of clay, pieces of weapons, bits of tools. He had never imagined that the job would be this taxing, or that there would be such a confusing jumble of unwanted cities built atop the Troy of Priam and Hector.

1871, 1872, 1873—Schliemann continued to dig. City after city came to light—seven in all, one atop the other, and then later two more. Nine Troys! And no way to tell how old they were, no way to determine which of the nine was the city of Priam. No treasure, no gold, came to light in any of them. Just a fantastic jumble of walls and debris, broken pottery, weapons, vases, household furnishings, that gave no clue. Schliemann had found a rich archaeological site, no doubt of it—but what was it?

Schliemann consulted Homer as his authority. The gods Poseidon and Apollo had built the walls of Troy, Homer said. And the Temple of Athena had been placed on the highest level of the city. So he reasoned that the temple would be somewhere in the middle of the mound, below the debris of later cities, and that the original walls would be at the bottom, near the level ground surrounding the hill. Priam's Troy must be near the bottom of the heap.

His discoveries as he burrowed toward the bottom were important ones, though they scarcely interested him. He wrote: "As it was my object to excavate Troy, which I expected to find in one of the lower cities, I was forced to demolish many interesting ruins in the upper strata; as, for example, at a depth of twenty feet below the surface, the ruins of a prehistoric building ten feet high, the walls of which consisted of hewn blocks of limestone perfectly smooth and cemented with clay." And in May, 1872, he uncovered a citadel of Homeric size, built of large blocks of limestone. But it was too close to the surface to be Trojan; it was actually of the time of Alexander the Great, Schliemann reasoned—seven centuries after the fall of Troy.

In the lower strata all was confusion. The layers overlapped, and in some places were missing entirely. But on the south side of the hill, 46 feet down, he came upon two different walls of enormous size. He called these the Great Tower. Digging near this tower in 1873, he broke through to a well-paved street, 17 feet wide, running downward into the depths of the mound. This, he decided, was a road leading into a large building, perhaps a palace. He set 100 men to work, and soon found the street full of ashes and burned bricks, indicating a fire in ancient times. And then he found the ruins of a large building composed of stones cemented with earth.

Always quick to jump to conclusions, Schliemann announced that the Great Tower was none other than the Scaean Gate, and the ruined building was the palace of Priam. Neither of them was quite big enough to equal Homer's description of them, but Schliemann was willing to ascribe the discrepancy to poetic license.

The scientific world, however, did not seem to take him

42

seriously, and Schliemann, wearied by his long labors, began at last to grow discouraged. He had found no treasure, no conclusive proof, merely a vast tangle of debris of many eras. Although in his own mind he was certain that the second city from the bottom was Priam's Troy, he had not found any objects that could definitely establish that fact. In May, 1873, he wrote to his brother that he was ending his digging and coming home: "We have been digging here for three years with a hundred and fifty workmen . . . and have dragged away 230,000 cubic meters of debris and have collected in the depths of Ilium a fine museum of very remarkable antiquities. Now, however, we are weary, and since we have attained our goal and realized the great ideal of our life, we shall finally cease our efforts in Troy on June 15th."

Then, on the day before digging was to be abandoned, a discovery was made, timed so dramatically that it almost seems hard to believe it happened this way. It was a hot morning, and the workmen were methodically shoveling spadefuls of dirt out of the excavation. Schliemann, although pessimistic and depressed, was supervising the workers in the faint hope that something worth while might turn up at the end of their labors.

They had gone down 28 feet at the wall around the building Schliemann called Priam's Palace, just northwest of the Scaean Gate. Schliemann peered into the dig, and suddenly his eyes widened in astonishment. What was that metallic object embedded under a layer of debris? Copper, he thought. And, behind the copper, something with the unmistakable yellow gleam of—

Of *gold!*

Schliemann was dumbstruck. Gold? Gold at last! For a long moment he could not speak. Then he forced himself to become calm, to think things through carefully. If the rascally workmen saw the gold, they might steal it. They might even murder Schliemann and Sophia to get the treasure. Who knew what these ignorant men might do for the sake of gold?

"Hurry!" Schliemann cried to Sophia. "Send the men home! Tell them to quit for the day."

"But it's still so early," the puzzled Sophia protested.

"Never mind that! Send them all back to the village. The overseer, too. Tell them they'll all get a full day's wages, that it's my birthday and they can go home to celebrate."

"But today isn't your birthday, Heinrich—"

"Send them away!" Schliemann shouted.

The workmen dispersed, smiling at their good fortune of an unexpected holiday. The moment they were gone, Schliemann told Sophia to fetch her red shawl. Together they jumped into the excavation.

"See?" he told her. "See here? Gold!"

He began to dig feverishly, jabbing at the ground with his knife. Sophia, at his side, helped him work. They were in constant danger, since digging out the treasure meant undermining the towering wall above them. Schliemann wrote afterward: "The wall of fortification, beneath which I had to dig, threatened every moment to fall down upon me. But the sight of so many objects, every one of which is of inestimable value to archaeology, made me reckless, and I never thought of any danger. It would, however, have been impossible for me to have removed the treasure without the help of my dear wife, who stood at my side, ready to pack the things I cut out in her shawl, and to carry them away."

Treasure after treasure came from the hole, until finally there was nothing more. Dizzy with success, flushed with triumph, Schliemann and Sophia climbed up and hurriedly returned to their cottage atop the hill. They hardly dared to speak until they were safely inside and the door locked. Then, breathless, they undid the shawl and let the glittering gold pour out.

It was an incredible hoard. The two finest objects were a pair of magnificent gold diadems of striking beauty. The larger was a fine gold chain, made to be worn around the crown of a woman's head. Seventy-four short and 16 longer gold chains hung from it, each consisting of 60 heart-shaped golden plates. The shorter chains would form a fringe on the wearer's brow; the longer ones, a golden covering for her shoulders. There were some 16,500 separate golden pieces altogether in the diadem. The smaller one was similar, but lacking the shoulder pieces. Both diadems were clearly the work of master artists; the gold was delicately and cunningly fashioned.

Besides these two, there were a gold bottle, six gold bracelets, a heavy golden goblet, 60 golden earrings, 8,700 small gold rings, perforated gold bars and buttons, bronze weapons, vases of silver and copper, and much else. Schliemann ran his fingers lovingly through the golden hoard, excited not so much by its value as gold—for he was many times a millionaire already—but because he believed it to be the actual treasure of Priam, king of Troy. With trembling hands he lifted the gleaming diadems and placed them on his wife's brow.

"Helen!" he cried. "You are Helen of Troy reborn!"

He was positive that this was Priam's treasure. He wrote: "Since I found all the objects together or packed into one another on the circuit wall, the building of which Homer ascribes to Neptune or Apollo, it seems certain that they lay in a wooden chest, of the kind mentioned in the *Iliad* as having been in Priam's Palace. It seems all the more certain, since I found close to them a copper key about four inches long, the head of which, about two inches in length and breadth, bears a very marked resemblance to the big key of an iron safe."

This object that Schliemann called a key actually turned out, upon close scrutiny by later investigators, to be a bronze chisel. Once again his impetuous nature had led him to a quick conclusion, and this time an incorrect one.

But he had settled in his own mind how the treasure had come to be where it was: "Some member of Priam's family," he wrote, "packed the treasure in the chest in great haste and carried it away without having time to withdraw the key, but was overtaken on the wall by the enemy or the fire, and had to leave the chest behind, where it was immediately covered to the depths of five or six feet with red ash and the stones of the neighboring Palace."

Schliemann had to abandon that pretty theory shortly afterward, when further digging revealed another treasure near the first cache, and three more a little farther away. It was unlikely that five different treasure-bearers had been forced to leave their hoards behind. Rather, Schliemann now came to believe, the chests had fallen from the burning palace.

Now that he had his treasure, he had to get it out of the country. He had originally received permission to dig by promising to hand half of everything he found over to the Turkish Government. But he could not bring himself to surrender the gold. He was sure that the corrupt, greedy Turks would simply melt the treasures down for their value as metal, rather than preserve them as relics of the past.

Schliemann managed to smuggle the treasure out of Turkey and into Greece. Safe in Athens, he announced his discovery. The angry Turks demanded that it be returned to them. At the orders of the Turkish ambassador, Schliemann's house in Athens was searched. But no treasure was found. Schliemann had prudently hidden it all in the homes and farms of Sophia's relatives.

✗ For the time being, Schliemann's archaeological career was halted. He wanted to go on to excavate Mycenae, the city of Agamemnon, in Greece. But the Greek government, mindful of the way he had smuggled his treasures out of Turkish territory, refused to give him a chance to try the same trick on them. He was told that he could not dig. It took him two years of haggling with the Government, and finally he was granted permission to excavate at Mycenae, provided that he handed over everything he found to Greek archaeologists.

While negotiating for the right to dig at Mycenae, Schliemann attempted to return to Troy for further work. But the Turks would not have him. They sued him, instead, for 10,000 francs as compensation for the antiquities he had stolen from Hissarlik. Schliemann willingly paid this, but still they would not let him return to his excavation. It was not until 1876 that the Turkish authorities permitted him to return to Troy.

But by that time he had succeeded in obtaining the right to work at Mycenae, and he chose to go there instead. He began digging there in August, 1876, and in a short while had made another spectacular discovery: a tomb containing several bodies and a treasure far beyond his findings at Troy. "I have found an unparalleled treasure of trinkets and jewels," Schliemann wrote. "All the museums in the world put together do not possess one-fifth of it." In his boyishly overenthusiastic way, he announced that he had located the actual tomb of Agamemnon himself—for who else would have been buried in Mycenae with such riches?

The triumphant Schliemann swept through the whole region of classical times, making discovery after discovery, and capping each with an extravagant announcement. He dug again at Troy in 1878 and 1879. The year 1880 saw him finding more treasure at a place called Orchomenus. In 1882 he dug again at Troy, and in 1884 at the city of Tiryns, where he unearthed an enormous palace. Then it was on to Crete, but his diggings there turned up little, and it fell to another man to make the great discoveries of Minos' kingdom. Schliemann died in 1890, to the last bursting with ambitious schemes.

Wherever he dug, this man found archaeological wonders. But had he truly found Troy? And had he found the tomb of Agamemnon? Or was he simply carried away by his poetic fancies?

Sadly, he was more wrong than right in most of his conclusions about his findings. Although he did find Troy for us, he guessed incorrectly about its actual position in the mound of Hissarlik. And, though Agamemnon lived about the twelfth century B.C., the tomb that Schliemann found at Mycenae was later identified as one of three to four centuries earlier. The dating is done by identifying pottery types, and the system of pottery dating had not come into being in Schliemann's time. It was only after many sites had been uncovered, all over the Greek peninsula, that a clear chronology of pottery types could be worked out, and dates given to the various styles.

In Schliemann's lifetime, scholars continued to deny that he had found Troy. Some insisted that Troy was not at Hissarlik at all; others were willing to concede that Hissarlik was the site, but not that Schliemann had identified the true Troy. Schliemann was plagued with bitter criticism and attack all his life, robbing him of much of the pleasure of his accomplishments.

In his later diggings at Troy, Schliemann brought distinguished scientists with him to help him in his work. The physician and amateur archaeologist Rudolf Virchow joined him, and then a brilliant young architect-archaeologist named Friedrich Dörpfeld, who supplied the gift for methodical scientific examination that the exuberant Schliemann lacked.

In 1880, Schliemann published an 800-page book on his Trojan excavations, called *Ilios*. In it he described the seven cities he had excavated at Hissarlik and advanced the theory that the second city from the bottom—the burned city in which he had found the treasure—was indeed Priam's Troy. But Schliemann had doubts himself, for once, and he voiced them worriedly in the book: "This petty little town, with its brick walls, which can hardly have housed 3,000 inhabitants . . . could [it] have been identical with the great Homeric Ilios of immortal renown, which withstood for ten long years the heroic efforts of the united Greek army of 110,000 men?"

But he doggedly maintained that the treasure he had found was the treasure of Priam. And if that was so, then the "petty little town" near the bottom of the heap had to be Priam's Troy. Schliemann was bothered by the situation, but could not resolve it to his satisfaction.

Virchow and Dörpfeld shared Schliemann's doubts, and they kept him from making any more grandiose declarations about the various cities of Hissarlik. And then new information came to light which convinced everyone—everyone but Schliemann—that the second city from the bottom could not be Priam's Troy.

First came the excavations at Mycenae. These turned up massive walls, as big as those Schliemann had found in the upper layers of Hissarlik. Schliemann had dated those walls as having been built in the time of Alexander the Great, around 300 B.C. But the walls at Mycenae were a thousand years older, by Schliemann's own admission—and yet architecturally they were similar. What was this? Were the Mycenaean walls younger—or the walls at Hissarlik older? For surely they came from the same era.

Dörpfeld began to suspect the truth—that the sets of walls at Mycenae and at Hissarlik both dated from about 1200 B.C., the time of the Trojan War, and that the city Schliemann thought was Troy was really a much older one. Confirmation came when Schliemann and Dörpfeld went on to excavate Tiryns. Here they uncovered a megaron, or hall. It had a pillared porch and a courtyard, and in all ways resembled a megaron described by Homer.

But at Hissarlik Dörpfeld had excavated a very similar megaron—in the sixth stratum from the bottom, the one that Schliemann insisted dated from 300 B.C. The truth was clear to everyone, now, but Schliemann remained blind to it. Priam had built his city atop an older, prehistoric one. The treasure that Schliemann had found was not Priam's at all, but the lost gold of some barbarian king who had ruled a thousand years before the events of the Trojan War.

Schliemann could not possibly accept this idea. He had too much of an emotional commitment to the notion that the city of the treasure was also the city of Priam. Dörpfeld's opinion, that Homeric Troy was the sixth city from the bottom, never rang true for Schliemann.

Just before the Second World War an archaeologist named Carl William Blegen came from America to study the Hissarlik site. He definitely established that there were nine separate settlements, one atop the other, and gave each a number. His work was more precise than Dörpfeld's, and though he too agreed that the upper city and not Schliemann's lower one was Homeric Troy, he identified it as the *seventh* from the bottom of the heap. The layer that was Homer's Troy is known as Layer VIIa, to dis-

76359

tinguish it from two upper layers of about the same era that had been built on the ruins of Priam's city.

Heinrich Schliemann achieved his life's ambition. He found Troy. He proved that there was solid historical truth behind Homer's wonderful stories. Although he was inaccurate and incorrect in many of his guesses, his basic work was undeniably invaluable. Later archaeologists were able to give more exact dates to the cities he found, and were able to give them their proper identifications.

Well, what of these Trojans, this vanished race of whom Homer sang? They are no myths; Schliemann proved that. But who were they? What were they like? Where did they come from, where did they go?

A century ago, no one could have answered those questions. Troy still lived in the shadowy realm of legend; it had no more reality than the Valhalla of the Norse myths, or the Atlantis of which Plato told. Today, though, decades of patient toil by archaeologists following in the footsteps of Schliemann have given us valid insight into the culture of Troy. There is still much that is unclear and perhaps never will be known. But the archaeologists have cleared away much of the mist and fog of antiquity.

The first cities sprang up in the East around 5000 B.C., in the fertile valley between the rivers Tigris and Euphrates. From this, the Cradle of Civilization, roving farmers spread out searching for new land. They entered Asia Minor about 3200 B.C. Near the coast, not many miles from the Dardanelles Strait that provided a sea route from the Aegean Sea to the Black Sea, they founded a city, which came to be known as Troy.

The city had a good location. It was situated directly on the main land route from Asia Minor to Europe and on the sea route through the Dardanelles. For fear of pirates, the

51

early settlers built their city some distance back from the sea, even though this meant an inconvenience for sea traders. This earliest Troy was built on a rocky hill, between two rivers that later Greeks would call the Scamander and the Simois. Strong walls were erected.

These early Trojans of 3000 B.C. were chiefly peasants and fishermen. They made little or no use of metal, and their tools were of stone and bone. They had stone axes and spears, and fishhooks of bone. Life was primitive; the people were simple. The women ornamented themselves with crude jewelry made of polished stones, leather, and bits of ivory. The people made pottery from clay, shaping it crudely by hand, and cutting uncomplicated geometric patterns into it. It was unpainted pottery, taking on the brown or black hues of the furnace.

Somewhere around 2600 B.C., this city fell. We do not know how it met its doom. Perhaps marauding pirates swept in from the sea, put the inhabitants to the sword, and burned the huts and shelters. For whatever reason, that earliest Troy perished, leaving behind it only crude fragments to indicate its existence.

But the site was a favorable one for a city, and perhaps only a decade or two after Troy I's downfall, a new town was constructed over the ruins of the old. This was a far larger and stronger city, with massive stone walls and large gates. The prince of Troy II had a fine palace, more than 50 yards wide. Its main room was large and rectangular, with a fireplace in the center, and the palace's walls, made of stone and mud, were a yard thick.

This was a more advanced civilization than that of Troy I. Metal-working was understood now—silver, lead, bronze, copper, and gold were all used. Pottery was now shaped on a potter's wheel, instead of with the bare hands, and it was richly ornamented with painted decorations.

Fig. 1. Roman Theatre near Pompeii, 1st century A.D.

All illustrations courtesy of the University Museum, University of Pennsylvania.

Fig. 2. Mural of a Boy, plastering a wall, Pompeii.

FIG. 3. Excavation of a Roman Theatre near Pompeii. Notice broken statue.

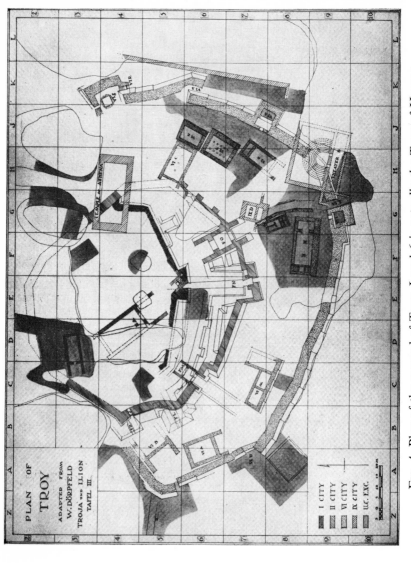

FIG. 4. Plan of the mound of Troy. Level 6 is actually the Troy of Homer

Fig. 5. Wall scene from Knossos. The Bull Dancers, possible source of the Minotaur legend.

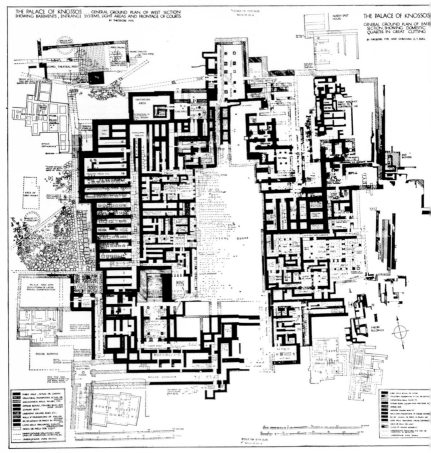

FIG. 6. Plan of the great palace of Knossos in Crete, the origin of the Labyrinth legend.

FIG. 7. Young nobles in a chariot. Wall scene from Tiryns in Greece.

Sir Austen Henry Layard   Ernest de Sarzec

Sir Henry C. Rawlinson   Georg Friedrich Grotefend

FIG. 8. Four famous unveilers of the Middle East and its past.

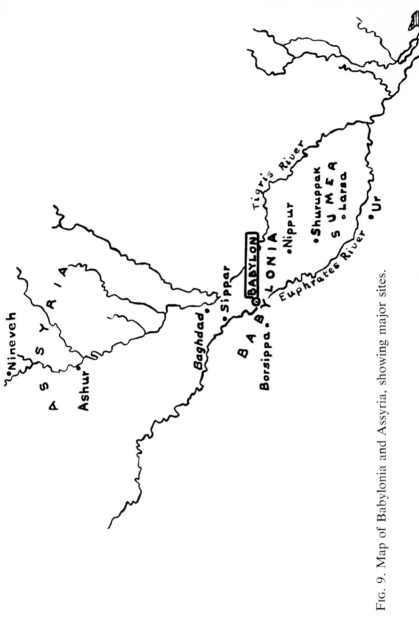

FIG. 9. Map of Babylonia and Assyria, showing major sites.

Fig. 10. The great ziggurat or pyramid of ancient Ur, rising from the surrounding desert.

Fig. 11. The famous Ishtar Gate of Royal Babylon, showing bulls and dragons.

Fig. 12. A relief of the Assyrian King, Ashurbanipal, showing the siege of a city.

FIG. 13. (*Top*) The ancient Mayan city of Uxmal, glimpsed over the surrounding jungle.

FIG. 14. (*Bottom*) The ruins of Palenque in Mexico, another remnant of Mayan greatness.

FIG. 15. A present-day Mayan village elder, seated on the ruins of
his ancestors' palaces.

Fig. 16. A relief of an ancient King of Angkor fighting the sea, like Canute of England.

FIG. 17. A carving of the Buddha, supported by adoring men and elephants, from Angkor Thom.

Leather jewelry gave way to jewelry of gold—arm bands, bracelets, pendants, diadems. The prince of the city dined on gold dishes. Even the unimportant people of the city owned gold jewelry, which they kept carefully stored in leather purses placed within pots of clay.

The first Troy had been a hunting and fishing community, but this second city was a center of commerce. It lay on the important trade route through the Dardanelles. Ships passing through the straits had to pay toll to Troy. Many merchants passed by, bringing raw metals and finished goods from the now old civilizations of Asia Minor to the new, rude, untutored peoples of Greece and northern Europe.

To protect its great wealth, Troy II built strong fortifications. Stone foundations 16 feet thick were laid around the city, and a sturdy wall of brick was placed above them. The gates were guarded heavily.

Yet the city's wealth must have made it a tempting target for attackers. About 2300 B.C., an army stormed Troy II, and neither gates nor walls could hold them back. We have no way of knowing who these invaders were. Perhaps they were a wandering tribe out of Europe, seeking a more favorable location for their city. Perhaps they were pirates, come ashore to loot and plunder. Or, it has been suggested, perhaps the men of Troy were so greedy for tolls that other cities united to destroy them.

No one knows. But this mighty second Troy fell, burned by the invaders. Much treasure was covered by falling debris as the city burned. It was this city that Schliemann thought was the Homeric Troy, for he was certain that such a wealth of gold could only be Priam's hoard. But Priam was a thousand years unborn when Troy II fell.

The great city had been destroyed, and for centuries afterward no one of consequence built on the site. Nomads came to live there, in flimsy huts of straw or brick. Once again the area was populated by hunters and fishers. From time to time the site was invaded again, or perhaps simply caught fire through accident, but there were always newcomers who would build over the ruins of what had gone before. Hundreds of years went by, and village succeeded unimportant village on the site of Troy. They have left only slight traces of their existence behind—a wisp of straw, a bit of shattered pottery.

Meanwhile, across the Aegean Sea in Greece, the westward move of civilization was continuing. The great city-building idea, which had moved outward from Mesopotamia in Asia, spread to Greece, and mighty walled cities sprang up at Tiryns, at Mycenae, and on the island of Crete. Soon these cities had reached the stage where they, too, could begin sending out merchants and explorers. Ships of Mycenae roved the whole Aegean area, and ventured far out into the Mediterranean. There was occasional warfare between the Greek cities when trade routes conflicted. There was no such concept as a nation. Each city stood alone and independent behind its massive walls. It sought its own trade routes, and its ships preyed as pirates on the ships of other cities.

While Mycenae and Tiryns flourished between the year 2000 B.C. and the year 1400 B.C., Troy—which had been a great city long before their birth—lay in ruins. But, about 1400, new settlers recognized the value of Troy's location, and they built another great city directly above the ruins of the old one. This was at least the sixth successive city to be built on the site, and it was to be the greatest —the Troy of Homer.

Troy VI was larger than Troy II had been. Again, it was ringed with a wall of stone and brick, topped with mighty towers and girdled with gates. The streets of the city were wide and handsome; the houses spacious and fine, with pillars supporting the roofs.

This was an active city, a wealthy city, whose importance far surpassed that of Troy II. That ancient Troy of 2500 B.C. had had its gold and its treasures, but the new city was even richer. Merchants came from all over Asia Minor to sell their wares, and to buy the goods produced by Trojan artisans. There were silversmiths and goldsmiths who manufactured jewelry of surpassing beauty; others fashioned weapons and tools from strong bronze; thin pottery, highly polished, was the equal of anything produced at Mycenae. The wealthy women of Troy decked their hair with ivory combs and preened themselves in mirrors of polished metal while their slaves took care of the dull burdens of household existence.

Unlike its predecessor, this wealthy city was able to defend itself against its attackers. But it could not protect itself against the elements. About the middle of the fourteenth century B.C., an earthquake shook Troy, shattering the great wall, toppling the fine houses. Once again the city had been destroyed.

But this time it was not abandoned. Survivors of the quake that had ruined Troy VI immediately began to rebuild on the same site, restoring the wall, re-erecting the towers. This rebuilt city, known to archaeologists as Troy VIIa, was the actual city of Priam. It was somewhat smaller than the city that had existed before the earthquake, but life in it was much the same as it had been before the cataclysm. Troy quickly regained its place in commerce, and the fame of its bronze implements and gold jewelry once again spread to every part of the civilized world.

Perhaps there was never a king named Priam; perhaps he was simply an invention of Homer's. But we now know that life in the walled city was much as Homer described it, and, if there never was a Priam, there was certainly "someone else of the same name" who ruled Troy. The king's palace was a splendid edifice of polished stone. There he lived with his queen and his many sons and daughters. Life in Troy was rich and pleasant. There were sports and games for the men, hunting, discus throwing, boxing, gambling with dice. The women danced, played catch, amused themselves with spinning and weaving. The nobles ate well, of fine meat and strong wine, served in vessels of gold and silver.

The Trojans dressed in garments of linen, dyed a deep purple, and in cooler weather donned robes made from the wool of black sheep. The men ornamented their hair with gold and silver spangles; the women wore elegant high-piled coiffures, heavy gold bracelets and necklaces, gleaming amber beads.

These Trojans were a powerful people. They resisted all enemy attacks. Elsewhere in Asia Minor, a warlike race called the Hittites tried without success to extend their dominion to that part of the peninsula ruled by Troy. And certainly pirates out of Greece made many vain attempts to raid the Trojan treasures. But Troy withstood these menaces.

About 1200 B.C., however, the many kings of Greece came to see that their unified might could topple Troy. For the first time in Greek history, the various cities ceased their quarrels with each other and formed a league against Troy, with Agamemnon, King of Mycenae, as the leader.

As mentioned previously, Homer tells us that the Trojan War started when Paris, son of Priam of Troy, stole Helen, the wife of Agamemnon's brother Menelaus, King of Sparta. Perhaps such a theft actually took place. We cannot say that it did, nor can we say that it was merely a story invented by a poet.

Whatever the truth of the story of Helen, we can be sure that the real motive for the outbreak of the war was something else indeed. Nothing so trivial as the theft of a king's wife would have induced the Grecian rulers to go to war against Troy. Greece was too scattered, too divided, for cities like Argos and Ithaca to care much about the fate of the Queen of Sparta.

But other reasons for the invasion existed—good reasons. Troy was a city of great wealth; conquering it would yield much booty, many slaves. And Troy was an annoying city, blocking the trade routes through the Dardanelles. Removing Troy would give ships of the Greek cities free access to Asia. And Troy was a business competitor, too, peddling its wares far and wide. Yes, there were many weighty reasons why the Greek kings would want to conquer Troy.

The expedition departed about 1190 B.C. Men from every city of Greece joined the armada; not only Mycenae and Sparta, the cities of Agamemnon and Menelaus, sent troops, but also Pylos, Argos, Ithaca, Crete, Rhodes, Tiryns —all the cities of this great age of Greece. Quite possibly the theft of Queen Helen was used as the pretext for starting the war.

But the Greeks—or rather, the Achaeans, as they called themselves then—found that starting the war was a good deal easier than winning it, for the Trojans were powerful enemies. Priam had assembled a great army, drawing men from the outlying districts of Asia Minor and even some from Thrace, on the mainland of Greece.

After much bloody battling, Agamemnon's forces gained a foothold on the beach near Troy. And there they remained for many years. Homer tells us that the siege lasted 10 years; perhaps this is a poet's exaggeration, perhaps not. The Achaeans had no machinery for breaching the Trojan walls. And, far from home, they were cut off from their supplies, and had to raid the cities around Troy for food.

Homer tells us that the long siege ended when Odysseus, shrewdest of the Achaeans, caused a great wooden horse to be built and left before the gates of Troy during the night. A Trojan priest discovered it, and the Trojans, thinking it a gift of the gods, brought it within the gates. But hidden within it were Achaean soldiers, who sprang out and opened the gates to Agamemnon's armies.

Whether or not Homer's story of the Trojan Horse is historical, we do know that Troy fell to the invaders about 1180 B.C. The city was sacked and burned once again and its population massacred. Troy was finished forever as a power in Aegean commerce and shipping.

But the plunderers returned to their homelands, and once again new builders appeared on the site. The few surviving Trojans erected another city, a pale shadow of what had been before. Archaeologists today call this city Troy VIIb 1. In it dwelt people of Trojan stock, living in poverty and telling tales of their former magnificence. Perhaps not all the surviving Trojans remained to resettle. Legend tells us that Aeneas, one of the greatest of Trojan heroes, went on to Africa, settling a while in Carthage, and then proceeded to Italy, where he married the daughter of a local chieftain and founded the race that would some day build Rome.

Troy VIIb 1 had a short life. Within a century or two, it was conquered by barbarians sweeping out of the Balkans. Other men came down out of the north to destroy the cities of Greece. A dark age came over the entire Mediterranean area, about 1000 B.C. In Greece, the golden era of the Achaeans ended bloodily, and the new men, the invaders who called themselves Dorians, would not again attain the heights reached by their predecessors for many centuries.

Asia Minor slipped into darkness. Greece gradually regained the prominence it had held before the downfall of the Achaeans. The Dorian Greeks slowly spread out beyond the seas about them. Troy, now settled by these latter-day Greeks, became a tourist attraction. Wealthy travelers could stop here to view the remnants of the city of Hector and Priam and Paris.

One of these sentimental visitors was Alexander the Great, in the fourth century B.C. Stopping off there in 334 B.C., Alexander worshiped at the Temple of Athena, and was shown weapons supposedly used in the Trojan War of 850 years earlier, including the shield of Achilles described by Homer. Alexander gave the town, which now bore the Greek name of Ilium, the rank of "city" once again, and exempted it from paying tribute to him in memory of its past greatness. After Alexander's death, his successor, Lysimachus, built a wall around Ilium five miles in circumference. Poor Schliemann, stumbling across the actual walls of Priam's city, mistook those for this wall of Lysimachus.

Schliemann's error is explained by the fact that, when Greek Ilium was built, the upper levels of the hill of Troy were cut away and demolished. Thus several strata are missing, representing the cities of about 900–600 B.C., and Priam's Troy was higher on the hill than Schliemann expected it to be. Only on the southern slope did these cities remain, and Schliemann was not aware of their existence.

Ilium, as strengthened by Lysimachus, was the head of a league of free Greek towns in Asia Minor for a quarter-century or so. But the city still retained its fatal attraction for invaders. The Gauls, those marauding barbarians out of western Europe, occupied Ilium in 278 B.C., but abandoned it 20 years later. It was reoccupied by Greeks, but once again attacked by Gauls in 218 B.C. This time the invaders were driven off.

None of Troy's former majesty remained. Ilium in the second century B.C. was a small, unimportant provincial town. A visitor, Demetrius of Scepsis, wrote of it that the houses "had not even roofs of tiles." But now a new nation had risen to world dominance: the Romans, who traced their ancestry back to Trojan Aeneas. For them, therefore, the site of Troy was a sacred place. Roman generals came to sacrifice at the Temple of Athena before important battles, and, as Novum Ilium, the city soon became a Roman possession. The dictator Sulla, he who had conquered Pompeii, carried out a lengthy rebuilding project at Novum Ilium in 85 B.C. The Emperor Caracalla visited the city in the second century A.D., sacrificing there as Alexander the Great had done 500 years before, and paying honors to the tomb of Achilles. By A.D. 400, the inhabitants of Novum Ilium were operating the place as a tourist attraction, manufacturing phony monuments of Priam's Troy. Then the Roman Empire crumbled, and the location of the city was forgotten. Turkish peasants settled there as the centuries passed, calling the mound Hissarlik.

No one today doubts that Hissarlik was the site of Troy. It lies between the Menderes (Scamander) and the Dumbrek Su (Simois) rivers. It matches the Homeric geography in every detail but that of the hot and cold springs, which of course may have dried out over the centuries.

The Trojans, then, were a businesslike and aggressive people who came out of Asia and repeatedly built important cities on the same site near the Strait of the Dardanelles. An invasion in 2300 B.C. put a halt to the city's expansion, but it was rebuilt some centuries later, survived an earthquake about 1350 B.C., and rose to an even more important position until sacked by the Achaeans in 1180. The Trojans struggled on for some years more, only to perish—along with Achaean Greece—beneath the assault of northern barbarians about 1000 B.C. After that, although the Trojan race was gone, other peoples (first Dorian Greek, and then Roman, and finally Turkish) dwelt on the site of Priam's mighty city. All this has been learned from the painstaking exploration of the layer upon layer of ruined cities—prehistoric Troy I, then Troy II of the golden treasure, Troy VI of the great walls, Troy VIIa of Priam's day, and the other strata.

And what of Homer, who sang of this great war and inspired Schliemann to find vanished Troy. Who was he? When did he live and write? Was he an eyewitness of the war?

We do not know, and perhaps will never know. Homer's origins are shrouded in myth, and we cannot dig to find the answer as Schliemann dug for Troy. Seven cities claim to be Homer's birthplace. Some authorities on the ancient world think that Homer was born as long ago as 1150 B.C.; others put him as late as 685 B.C. In the one case, he was born while some heroes of the Trojan War still lived, and so could have assembled a reasonably accurate account of it; in the other, he was simply retelling a story that had come down over a period of 400 years, with all the distortions and alterations that four centuries of word-of-mouth retelling quite naturally would create.

Quite probably Homer lived about 800 or 900 B.C.—after the downfall of the Achaean Greeks, but several centuries before the time of Herodotus, Plato, Socrates, and the other known figures of historical times. His poems, therefore, were almost certainly drawn from distorted accounts of the Trojan War. In all likelihood, the story of Achilles and Hector had come down from one sage to the next, until Homer finally codified the stories into their present form. Some elements of the poems undoubtedly are of historical accuracy; others are probably additions made by imaginative storytellers a century or two after the war.

The works of Homer were recited orally long before they were ever written down. No doubt other changes slipped into the story this way. By 500 B.C. several different texts existed, some of them quite different from others. In 150 B.C. Aristarchus of Samothrace, head of the famous library at Alexandria, prepared the text that we have today.

Homer sang of an age of heroes that actually existed several centuries before his own birth. His poems are a mixture of fact and fantasy—but there was enough fact in them to enable Heinrich Schliemann to go to a place like the one Homer described, dig there, and there locate the ruins of Priam's fabled city of Troy.

3

Knossos of Crete

Heinrich Schliemann had found Troy and Agamemnon's Mycenae, had located the golden
city of Orchomenus, had excavated the colossal
citadel at Tiryns, legendary birthplace of Her-
cules. Wherever he went, he uncovered traces
of an important and powerful civilization that had existed
around the Aegean Sea between 2000 and 1000 B.C.

The center of this civilization, which we now know as
the Minoan-Mycenaean civilization, was, Schliemann was
certain, the island of Crete. Every legend indicated that
Crete had been the home of a mighty people even before
the cities of Mycenae and Tiryns had risen to prominence.
The myths talked of Minos, the great king of Crete, whose
capital was the city of Knossos. The Greek historian
Thucydides, writing in the fifth century B.C., reported
that "Minos is the earliest ruler we know of who possessed
a fleet, and he controlled most of what are now Greek
waters. He ruled the Cyclades [a group of islands in the
Aegean Sea] and was the first colonizer of most of them,
appointing his own sons as governors. He cleared the sea
of pirates, as far as he could, to secure his own revenues."

A legend has it that one of Minos' sons was the Minotaur, half-bull and half-man, and to contain this fierce creature Minos had the architect Daedalus build the maze of passages known as the Labyrinth. And to Knossos came the hero Theseus to brave the Labyrinth, kill the Minotaur, and escape with Minos's daughter Ariadne. Another myth says that Zeus himself, chief of all the gods, was born on Crete. Homer told of Idomeneus, a great king of Crete descended from Minos. If the old tales held any truth, there had been a great civilization on Crete, perhaps the greatest in the whole Aegean area.

Little archaeological work had been done there before Schliemann's time. The site that was supposed to be that of ancient Knossos contained only the foundations of Roman ruins of relatively recent times. A hill in the area, known as "The Gentleman's Head," did contain large ruined walls made of gypsum blocks, covered with inscriptions in a language no one could read. But no digging had been done there.

Fresh from his triumphs at Troy, Mycenae, Orchomenus, and Tiryns, Schliemann came to Crete in 1886, at the age of 64, after having spent three years obtaining permission to dig. Crete was then a Turkish possession; it is a large island lying in the Mediterranean almost equidistant from Greece and Turkey.

Getting permission from the authorities was one thing—getting permission from the owner of the Kephala, or Gentleman's Head, was another matter entirely. The land was owned by a foxy Cretan who refused to sell only the Kephala. If Schliemann wanted to buy, he was told, he would have to buy the entire property, including 2,500 olive trees, for the considerable sum of 100,000 francs.

"I'll give you 40,000," Schliemann countered.

There was a protracted session of dickering, continuing over several years, and finally the owner agreed to sell for

40,000 francs. But Schliemann checked the trees in the olive grove and found not 2,500 but 888. Outraged at this attempt to cheat him, he angrily called off the deal. For once, his businessman's instincts triumphed over his archaeological zeal.

He still dreamed of finding Knossos, calling the project the one great piece of work that would crown his career. But that was in 1889, and the next year he was dead, with Knossos still unpurchased and unexcavated.

The task of uncovering the city of King Minos fell to a shortsighted, soft-spoken Englishman named Arthur Evans, who had visited Schliemann in Athens in 1882. Then, Schliemann had shown the young Evans seals and signet rings he had found in Mycenae. The objects had fascinated Evans; they seemed definitely Greek in character, yet had an alien quality, reminding him of the Egyptian and Assyrian art forms. Evans' interest in the pre-Homeric civilizations of the Aegean was kindled permanently at that meeting.

Evans and Schliemann were alike in only three ways: they were both rich men, they both had a consuming passion for archaeology, and they were both stubborn and egotistical. But where Schliemann was flamboyant, impetuous and dashing, Evans was quiet, scholarly and reserved. Schliemann was a self-educated businessman, whose fortune was self-made; Evans had been an outstanding student at Oxford and at the German University at Göttingen, and had inherited his wealth from his father. While Schliemann carried on a perpetual war with other archaeologists, Evans was deeply respected by his colleagues and received many honors from them.

Evans was born in 1851—the year Schliemann was off in California profiting from the gold rush. His family owned a paper-manufacturing firm, and Arthur grew up in an environment of wealth and scholarship. His father was a geologist and collector of antiquities, and their home was filled with cases of flint and bronze artifacts of prehistoric origin that the Evanses had found in trips through Britain and France. Arthur's special interest was in ancient coins and seals. His sister wrote of him that he "was extremely shortsighted, and a reluctant wearer of glasses. Without them, he could see small things held a few inches from his eyes in extraordinary detail, while everything else was a vague blur. Consequently the details he saw with microscopic exactitude, undistracted by the outside world, had a greater significance for him than for other men."

As a young man he enjoyed travel, by foot or by horse, and roved Europe in search of the coins, seals, and antiquities that interested him. When he was 20 he visited the rough Balkan countries, then under Turkish occupation. He became an expert on complex Balkan politics, writing a book on the now forgotten provinces of Bosnia and Herzegovina in 1876 (they are parts of Yugoslavia today). He served as a newspaper correspondent in the Balkans after the Austrians replaced the Turks as rulers there, and while interviewing revolutionaries and touring prison camps he had time to explore medieval castles, excavate Roman ruins, and study ancient inscriptions.

In 1878, he returned to England and married Margaret Freeman, a girl of his own scholarly nature whom he had met while at Oxford. Typically, they celebrated their engagement by visiting a London exhibit of antiquities from Troy, newly discovered by Dr. Heinrich Schliemann.

After his marriage, it was back to Bosnia as a newspaper correspondent, and more excavation of Greek and Roman ruins. Expelled by the Austrian authorities because he was too openly sympathetic with the nationalistic Bosnian revolutionaries, he toured Greece, meeting Schliemann and developing his fascination for pre-Homeric antiquities of the Mycenaean era. After visiting the excavations at Tiryns and Mycenae, he returned to England to become Keeper of the Ashmolean Museum. Whenever he wearied of his museum duties, he traveled, dug, bought ancient coins, and studied them in great detail.

In 1893, Margaret Evans died. Evans, to console himself, plunged ever deeper into archaeology. While staying in Athens he came upon some peculiar stones engraved with an unfamiliar kind of writing, and, studying the inscriptions with his peculiar high-powered vision, he saw that they were unlike any he had known elsewhere.

"Where are these stones from?" he asked the dealer in antiquities who had offered them to him.

"They are from Crete," he was told.

Evans resolved to go to Crete as soon as possible. Perhaps he would find more of these odd seal stones there, he told himself, or even a clue to their origin. In the spring of 1894, he landed at Herakleion, Crete.

He went to the Kephala, a few miles from the city. The landlord who had made so much trouble for Schliemann was more willing to sell now, and Evans purchased some of the land around the site. He explored without digging, hoping to find more of the little seal stones with the strange inscriptions. The great gypsum walls, partly visible on the site, aroused his interest. Soon he was making plans to conduct a full-scale excavation at the Kephala.

The Turks left Crete in 1896. Evans returned, bought the rest of the site, and obtained official backing from the King of Greece for his project. In 1900, he began to dig, expecting to spend a year—18 months at most—at the excavation. He was 49 then, and no doubt he would have been surprised to learn that he was destined to spend the remaining 41 years of his long life exploring the kingdom of Minos!

Almost at once he began to make discoveries. The ruins at Knossos lay only a few feet below the surface; there had been no overbuilding through the centuries, as at Troy. The astonishing thing was that the artifacts he was turning up were neither Greek nor Roman; they were of great age, obviously pre-Homeric, even pre-Mycenaean.

Earlier diggings at the roughly quadrangular mound of Knossos had turned up some big jars of clay, called pithoi, and some good-sized walls. But Evans was not prepared for the magnitude of what he found within the first few weeks of his excavating. There was no golden treasure such as Schliemann had discovered. Rather, there was a palace, of such colossal size as to dwarf even the massive buildings at Mycenae. It was clearly the work of a genius of an architect—and one who had lived perhaps a thousand years before the Trojan War!

As the digging continued, more of the vast building came to light. Soon Evans had uncovered 5½ acres of palace grounds, built on a truly regal scale. The clear indication was that Crete had been the center of this ancient Mycenaean culture, and that Mycenae and Tiryns, with their smaller buildings, had been mere provincial settlements.

The palace seemed endless. It was built about a gigantic rectangular courtyard, and a confusing network of other rooms radiated from it on all sides. It was a genuine labyrinth, of great size and startling antiquity. The project that Evans had thought could be concluded in a year or a year and a half now showed itself to be a life's work.

Part of the confusion of the floor plan stemmed from the fact that several palaces had been built on the site. Later builders had demolished some of the earlier rooms and had tacked on additions of their own. The site had clearly been inhabited continuously for 15 or 20 centuries, and over so great a span of time the palace had grown extremely complicated in design. Even after 25 years of continuous work, Evans regarded the place as a tangled maze.

His first interest was in the bricks and clay tablets covered with the mysterious Cretan hieroglyphics. There was no way of deciphering this script, but Evans hoped that a key would be found as he dug deeper. The architectural complexity of the palace awed him, but he concentrated on the hieroglyphics.

Then, in April, 1900, a wall painting was discovered— a fresco, painted directly on the stone. It showed a young man holding a high, funnel-shaped cup of the Mycenaean style. Evans noted in his diary: "The figure is life size, the flesh color of a deep reddish hue. . . . The profile of the face is a noble type; full lips, the lower showing a slight peculiarity of curve below. The eye is dark and slightly almond shaped. . . . The arms are beautifully modelled. The waist is of the smallest . . . it is far and away the most remarkable human figure of the Mycenaean age that has yet to come to light."

The fresco had an unearthly beauty and freshness about it. Evans' workingmen bowed before it as though it were the portrait of some unknown saint.

Soon afterward came an even more exciting find: the throne room of Minos himself. Evans had been digging along the ground floor of the palace, in the western wing, and had worked his way down a long corridor off which were many small storage rooms. On April 13, 1900, he entered a rectangular room that he thought at first was a bath chamber. But there was no drain for the escape of bath water, and further digging revealed a seat of throne-like design along the north wall. Here, clearly, was the seat where King Minos dispensed justice, 2,000 years before the birth of Christ.

As they continued to clear the debris from the rooms, fresco after wondrous fresco came to light. A fresco of people in solemn procession, another of a boy, others showing strange griffin-like creatures. Then a great painting of a charging bull.

Again and again bulls were seen, on the walls, on seal rings, carved into blocks of stone. "What a part these creatures play here!" Evans exclaimed.

He remembered the legends of the Minotaur, the Bull of Minos. The old story told of how Minos, master of Knossos, had sent his son Androgeus to Athens as a contestant in the games. Androgeus had easily beaten the Athenians in the games, and they jealously murdered him at the order of Aegeus, the Athenian king. Furious, Minos sent his fleet to conquer Athens and imposed a terrible vengeance upon them. Each year, Minos commanded, the Athenians would have to send seven of their finest young men and seven of their fairest maidens in tribute to Knossos. There, they would be sacrificed to the Minotaur, the raging bull that Minos' wife had borne and who was kept penned up in the Labyrinth of Daedalus.

After 28 of Athens' young people had perished in this way, the hero Theseus, son of Aegeus, returned to Athens from a long journey and learned of Minos' harsh vengeance.

"Let me go to Knossos as one of the seven youths this year," Theseus asked his father. "I'll kill the Minotaur and put an end to our city's shame."

Aegeus was fearful of letting his son go, but Theseus insisted, and when the tribute ship put to sea Theseus was aboard. The ship had black sails, in mourning for the 14 young lives it carried to death in Knossos. Theseus told his father that he would replace the black sails with white ones if he returned alive and successful from his mission.

In Knossos, the 14 captives were shown to Minos, and when Ariadne, Minos' daughter, saw Theseus, she fell in love with him. That night she came to him in the dungeon where he lay. She offered him a sword and a ball of thread.

"With this sword, you can slay the Minotaur," she told him. "And be sure to unravel this thread as you enter the Labyrinth. That way you can retrace your path and escape from the maze!"

Theseus entered the Labyrinth armed with the sword and let out the ball of thread while Ariadne held the other end. In a bloody battle, he killed the monster and traced his way out of the Labyrinth by following the thread.

The 14 young Athenians escaped successfully from Knossos, taking Ariadne with them. But so excited were they over their triumph that they forgot to change their ship's sails from black to white. As the black-sailed ship drew near Athens, King Aegeus, watching from his window, saw it and thought that his son Theseus was dead. He cast himself into the sea in his grief—and it has been known as the Aegean since that day.

The legend of Theseus and the Minotaur was widely accepted throughout Greece even in fairly sophisticated times. A certain ship kept at Athens was considered to be the actual one in which Theseus had sailed, and once a year this ship was sent to the city of Delos bearing special sacrifices. While the ship was away, Athens remained in a state of solemnity. Indeed, the execution of Socrates was postponed for 30 days until the return of the sacred ship, for no execution could be carried out while the ship was at Delos.

There seemed to be, then, something more than mere fantasy in this legend of Theseus and the Minotaur. Something, Evans thought, had to account for the uncanny hold this myth had on the later Greeks.

At Tiryns, Schliemann had found a painting of a huge bull with an athlete clinging to his horns. No one had offered any explanation of the work. Now, at Knossos, Evans came upon a truly spectacular fresco, one of the masterpieces of ancient art. It showed a bull and three toreadors, a young man and two girls, all slim-waisted and broad-shouldered, in what was the now-familiar classic Cretan style. The lean, agile boy was shown in the act of performing a somersault over the back of the charging bull. He is in mid-air, tumbling heels over head, while behind the bull one of the girls waits to catch him. The other girl is apparently about to perform the same dangerous somersault; she has caught hold of the bull's fierce horns, and seems just ready to spring into the air and make the backflip. The painting tingles with excitement. Looking at it, one can all but hear the snort of the bull, the exultant cry of the boy as he does his death-defying backroll.

Again and again throughout the palace, this strange scene was repeated: elegant, noble young boys and girls vaulting over the sharp horns of an enormous bull. Was this, Evans wondered, a representation of the legendary sacrifice of the Athenian captives? Was it a ritual sacrifice, with the hostages forced to perform these backflips until the bull gored or trampled them to death?

Certainly there had to be a kernel of truth in the Theseus legend, Evans reasoned. The palace, with its twisting corridors and hidden staircases, was clearly a labyrinth. The Minotaur had been no half-human monster, but simply a giant bull to whom hostages from the Greek cities were sacrificed. And the story of Theseus was symbolic of the eventual overthrow of the Minoan kings by the Greeks, who invaded Knossos and destroyed the great palace.

Later, Evans offered a different explanation. There had been no hostages, no invasion of Knossos by the Greeks. Rather, the palace of Minos had been shaken by a tremendous earthquake and had been abandoned by the Cretans. Many years later, after the glory of Knossos had passed, wandering seamen from Athens had visited Greece. They had come upon the ruined palace, had explored its tangled passageways, had come across the exciting paintings of young people leaping over the backs of bulls.

The paintings may have depicted some religious ritual in Minoan life, Evans theorized, rather than any sacrifice of captives. Possibly young priests had had to leap over bulls as part of their initiation into the priesthood. But the Greek visitors, superstitious and awed by the majesty of the wrecked palace, had concocted their own explanation. They had invented a story of a maze, of a giant bull-monster, of captives sent as tribute. They brought their story back to Athens, where it was accepted and took firm hold in the imaginations of the people, until it became as real to them as the stories of Homer.

Evans continued to dig and to restore the vast palace of Minos, and each year new wonders emerged. He now had a fairly good idea of how the palace must have looked in its years of glory. Its walls must have been decorated in many colors, and so the many-storied building would have glittered blazingly in the Cretan sunshine. Within, all was of the utmost luxury. Some 17,000 gallons of precious oil were stored in jars in the palace's rooms, and untold treasure. Crete was a commercial center in its heyday, greater even than Troy. So powerful was the Minoan fleet that there was no need even to build fortifications about the palace.

Evans uncovered the domestic part of the palace, where the queen had reigned. It was a gay, airy quarter, well ventilated, well lighted. Spiral ornaments and dolphins at play were depicted on the walls. Nearby was the palace workshop, where oil was pressed, wine was made, pottery was fashioned.

Across the courtyard, on the western side, were the public rooms. Here the city elders met, here the king delivered his decrees, here merchants from afar sold their wares to the royal procurers.

The palace was lavishly decorated. Inset in the walls were fragments of decorative material—gold foil, sparkling crystal, porcelain of bright green hue, blue lapis lazuli. The accent throughout the huge building was on color, life, comfort. Everything was designed for beauty, and painted vividly. The king's game board was found, a wonderful thing of crystal and ivory and gold and silver.

There were temples on the western side of the palace, too. Gypsum blocks were marked with the sign of the Labrys, or Double Ax, the insignia of the Minoan goddess. This sign was repeated throughout the palace, as the cross might be used in a Christian land. The worship of this goddess was, Evans thought, coupled with worship of the king as a living god. Minos—the name must have descended from king to king for centuries—was a god in his own lifetime, and after his death, legend said, the original Minos had been appointed one of the three judges of Hades.

The amazing thing about this glittering palace was its architectural brilliance. It was as big as Buckingham Palace in London, and surely must have been the greatest work of architecture of its day. It had splendid bathrooms with extraordinarily clever sanitary arrangements. There were drains and ventilators, conduits for water, many incredible engineering accomplishments. It was hard for Evans to keep in mind that this palace had been built thousands of years before his day, and had not been in use since about 1400 B.C. Everywhere, vivid paintings showed smiling Cretans going about the sophisticated pleasures of life in a very modern way. The women were dressed in modern-looking, stylish gowns; the men were handsome, athletic, smiling. Paintings showed the nobles of the court at the theater, at sports, at parties and feasts.

Evans dug up hundreds of tablets, too, which seemed to record at great length the thoughts and beliefs of these Minoans. Sadly, though, he was defeated at the task of translating them. There was no way even to begin. The strange hieroglyphics resembled nothing else in the world, and so the thoughts of the Minoans remained forbidden to him. He could never know the history, the poetry, the ideas of these gay people whose portraits he saw throughout the palace.

By the end of 1900, Evans was beginning to reconstruct the history of these vanished people. He wrote: "The realms of the legendary Minos, the great conqueror and law-giver who at the close of his temporal reign took his seat on the dread tribunal of the netherworld, the abode of Daedalus, the father of architecture and plastic arts, the haunt of the mysterious Dactyls, the earliest artificers in iron and bronze . . . the birthplace of Zeus himself, Crete was in remote times the home of a highly developed culture which vanished before the dawn of history."

In 1901, accompanied by his 77-year-old father, Evans dug deeper, finding the Grand Staircase, the single most impressive architectural achievement of the palace. He realized that he was only just coming to the real center of the palace's buildings. And more wonderful frescoes came to light. Evans described one, showing two women at a shrine, this way: "The lively nature of the conversation at once strikes the eye. [One woman] points her statement by thrusting forward her right arm so as almost to lay her hand on the other's lap while her confidante raises hers in amazement—'You don't say so!'. . . . These scenes of feminine confidence, of tittle-tattle and society scandals, take us far away from the productions of classical art in any age. Such lively genre and rococo atmosphere bring us nearer to quite modern times."

Evans and other dedicated archaeologists worked at Knossos and nearby sites for decades. Continuing work began to provide a series of dates for the Knossian relics. An odd parallel to Egyptian history began to present itself.

Ancient Egyptian history is divided into three great eras—the Old Kingdom, the Middle Kingdom, and the New Kingdom, beginning at about 3200 B.C. and ending in 332 B.C. when Egypt passed into the twilight of its days under foreign domination. The dates of the Egyptian eras are fairly well certain, thanks to many documents that have been recovered. The Old Kingdom endured till about 2100 B.C.; it was the era of the great builders of pyramids. The Middle Kingdom (2100–1700 B.C.) was a time of expansion rather than of monument building. In 1700 B.C., Egypt was conquered by an Asiatic people known as the Hyksos, who ruled for 150 years. The Hyksos were expelled in 1555 B.C., and the New Kingdom began. This was the era of the great Pharaohs, Rameses and Tuthmosis and Akhnaten, and it was also the time of the exodus of the Israelites from Egypt.

Early in his excavations, Evans found in the palace an Egyptian statue that was identified as a Middle Kingdom work of the Twelfth Dynasty (2000–1790 B.C.). This gave Evans an approximate date for the Knossian objects found on that level of the excavation. As the work went on, Evans was able to match other datable Egyptian objects found on the sites to Cretan objects surrounding them, and through this means was able to establish a series of dates for the

Minoan objects going as far back as 3200 B.C. The process was cross-checked when Minoan objects were found in Egypt. Evidently there had been trade between Crete and Egypt from the very earliest days. Since archaeologists were fairly certain of the age of Egyptian objects, they now knew how old each layer of the Minoan finds was.

Having dated his finds, Evans went on to work out a grand scheme of Minoan history. Crete, too, he said, had had an Old, a Middle, and a New Kingdom, roughly corresponding to the Egyptian ones. The Old, or Early Minoan Kingdom, had lasted from about 3000 B.C. to about 2000 B.C.; the Middle Minoan Kingdom had lasted from 2000 to 1600 B.C.; and the New, or Late Minoan, had had the shortest life of all, from 1600 B.C. to 1400 or 1350 B.C. It was a story of a gradual rise to glittering dominion, followed by sudden catastrophe.

The ancestors of the Minoans, Evans theorized, came to Crete somewhere about 4000 B.C. They probably came from the Middle East, from Syria and the surrounding regions. From very early times these people had contact with Egypt, where an unusually advanced civilization had already developed. In 3200 B.C., Menes, first of the great Pharaohs, conquered all of Egypt, and it is quite likely that refugees fled to Crete, bringing with them the influence of Egyptian culture. The newcomers taught the original Asian people new arts of stoneworking and jewelry-making, and new methods of agriculture as well.

During the thousand years of the Early Minoan Period, civilization developed on the island. Pottery and painting were perfected. Metalwork, though, was still beyond the Minoans, nor were they yet expert sculptors. The island was divided into at least three groups, independent of each other. Knossos had already been settled, but it had not yet attained dominance on the island.

During the Middle Minoan Period, Knossos became the capital of the island. This was the golden age of Crete. The first Minos ruled then, and under his sway Crete became one of the wealthiest lands in the world. The use of metals was introduced; sculpture attained perfection; the art of fresco painting was brought to dazzling proficiency. The Cretan aristocracy lived a life of pleasure and amusement, made rich by commerce and industry. During this period, the inscribed seal stones that Evans was to find so interesting were brought to their highest beauty and complexity. And architecture, too, was mastered. The great palace of Minos was built, with all its miraculous features of design, its drainage system, and its ventilation.

Crete enjoyed not only prosperity but also peace. Isolated by the sea, it was safe from all attack, for it had the strongest navy in the world. A Minoan empire developed, as the Minoans established trading posts first on one Aegean island, then the next. Ultimately, they held control over the entire Aegean region.

During this period, too, the mainland cities of Mycenae and Tiryns sprang up and flourished. Their styles of architecture and sculpture were similar to those of Knossos, but on a smaller scale. Evans believed that Mycenae and Tiryns were colonies of Crete, and were dominated politically by it. Other authorities take a different stand: that the mainland people were an entirely different race, the Achaeans, who imitated the older and greater culture of the Minoans. They remained independent of Crete, but hired Minoan artists to design their buildings and produce works of art for them.

About 1750 B.C., at the height of the Middle Minoan Period, an earthquake shook the island. The great palace suffered heavily. But the Minoans set to work and rebuilt it more grandly than before. In 1570 B.C., an earthquake once again destroyed the palace. Whole sections were buried, not to be uncovered until the spades of Evans' workmen touched the site. Stone blocks weighing more than a ton were hurled 20 feet and more from the palace walls.

But the Minoans restored what they could and built directly atop what was too heavy to move. Now the Late Minoan Period had begun. The expansion of the Middle Kingdom culminated now, with Crete a world power on a scale with Egypt. From his mighty palace at Knossos, the Minoan king ruled a far-flung dominion of islands and colonies. Excellent roads crisscrossed Crete. The glory of Crete was world renowned. Minoan ships were in every port, bearing goods manufactured in the workshops at Knossos. Crete was at the pinnacle of its power. The arts flourished, and the Cretan aristocracy lived in unparalleled magnificence.

Then, in 1400 B.C., destruction came once again. Almost overnight the power of Crete was snuffed out. Not only Knossos but also the other important cities of the island were destroyed, and Crete vanished from the roll of powerful nations.

How did it happen? What sudden cataclysm overwhelmed the land of Minos?

The story is shrouded in confusion, and several conflicting versions are held by different archaelogical schools. All agree on only one thing: that, about 1400 B.C., the Cretan civilization met its doom with stunning rapidity.

Arthur Evans believed that it had been an earthquake that shook the island and demolished the great cities. He had already uncovered evidence of two earthquakes before the last catastrophe, in 1750 B.C. and again in 1570 B.C. And in recent years, when records have been kept of such things, Crete had been known to have a particular susceptibility to earthquakes. One, at the city of Candia in 1856, had wrecked all but 18 out of 3,620 houses.

In 1926 Evans himself experienced a Cretan earthquake. It began at 9:45 in the evening; he was quietly reading when the building he was in began to shake and groan, and the ground trembled and gave off a sound that Evans said was "like the muffled roar of an angry bull." In only 75 seconds, the town of Candia was once again nearly destroyed. The Palace of Minos had survived the quake unharmed, because Evans had poured a fortune into strengthening it with concrete and hidden steel girders against just such a happening. This personal experience of an earthquake left Evans utterly sure that the island had been devastated in 1400 B.C. not by enemy invaders but by a severe earthquake.

Other students of archaeology prefer the invasion theory. They point out that the ruins were not only shaken up, but showed signs of having been burned. There was no reason why an earthquake should have caused fire. And, since the Cretans had recovered from earlier quakes, they could well have rebuilt after this one—if not for the fact that they had been set upon by invaders from the mainland. Twice Knossos succumbed to earthquake damage, and recovered; the third time, the quake was followed by armed marauders, and the kingdom fell.

But who were these marauders?

Again, opinion differs. One branch thinks that Crete, Mycenae, and Tiryns were all inhabited by the same race, a dark-skinned people. Mycenae and Tiryns, this theory holds, were colonies planted by the Minoans.

About 2000 B.C., then, a race of light-skinned people came marching down out of the north. These were the Achaeans. The Achaeans were barbaric and nomadic, but they were many in number. They attacked the mainland cities of Mycenae and Tiryns.

These were cities with great walls. The walls at Mycenae were 46 feet thick, those at Tiryns 57 feet thick. For many years, this theory goes, the Minoan colonists at Mycenae and Tiryns defended themselves successfully against the Achaean barbarians from the north. But as the centuries passed, the light-skinned Achaeans developed the skills of civilization and finally conquered the citadels of the dark-skinned people of Mycenae and Tiryns.

Solidifying their hold on the mainland, the warlike Achaeans next cast their eyes on the mother country of the dark-skinned people, the island of Crete. Crete was confident of its ability to defend itself through its navy, and so had not bothered to build any walls around its cities. The Achaeans invaded, about 1400 B.C. Perhaps their invasion came right after a disastrous earthquake on Crete. The Minoans were unable to cope with the double catastrophe of earthquake and invasion, and they fell before the Achaean swords. The fair-skinned men burned the cities of the Minoans and smashed the power of Crete forever.

The other theory says that the people of Mycenae and Tiryns were never of Cretan stock. Rather, they were Achaeans who imitated the ways of the older civilization of Crete, learning the Minoan arts and skills, until finally they dared to rise up and destroy the ancient Cretan kingdom.

Whatever the explanation, whether earthquake or barbarians from the north or both, we know that the power of the Minoans ended about 1400 B.C. For the next three or four hundred years, it was the Achaeans who dominated the region, just as the Cretans had before them. Mycenae became the most important city, and the Achaean peoples traded with Egypt and the Orient, replacing the Cretans as masters of the sea. With Crete gone, the new rival of the Achaeans was Troy, as we have told—and, about 1180 B.C., the Achaeans under Agamemnon of Mycenae destroyed Troy as they had destroyed Crete.

And then it was the turn of the Achaeans themselves to know destruction. Grown fat and lazy with triumph after triumph, they fell before a new wave of barbarian invaders from the north, the Dorians, who conquered the cities of Mycenae and Tiryns. It would be centuries before these Dorians could reach the heights attained by the Achaeans —but, after a Dark Age lasting four centuries or more, the Dorians did indeed attain a great civilization, the civilization of Plato and Pericles and Sophocles.

Conqueror after conqueror, civilization after civilization—this is the story of the troubled Aegean area. The work of many archaeologists has brought back to life this wonderful tale, showing the successive rise and fall of the Minoans, the Achaeans, the Dorians. And, of course, it was Homer, a poet of the Dorian conquerors, who sang of the legendary heroes of the Achaean era which the Dorians had ended.

Crete passed permanently from power when it fell in 1400 B.C. When the Dorians visited it, five or six hundred years later in the time of Homer, they found only ruins, the already half-buried shell of the palace of Minos. Perhaps then they saw the frescoes of youths and maidens vaulting over bulls, and the tales these Dorian seamen told evolved into the legend of Theseus and the Minotaur, with Theseus seen as an Achaean hero who led the conquest of the kingdom of Minos.

The story is a tangled one, and sorting fact from fancy is no simple job. The large patterns of the story are known: that the Cretans had a great civilization that ended suddenly and speedily in 1400 B.C., that the Achaeans of whom Homer sang rose next to power, and that the Dorian invaders succeeded them a century or two after the Trojan War. But the details, the smaller incidents, are still hidden in the sands of time.

The answer to the riddles of Crete, Evans felt, might be contained in the many written accounts found in the palace at Knossos. No less than 1900 clay tablets turned up in the ruins, inscribed in the mysterious symbols no one could read. It was this language that had first brought Evans to Crete, long before he dreamed of uncovering an entire civilization. Yet when he died in 1941, at the age of 90, it was still impossible to understand anything the Minoans had written. Their books were sealed by our ignorance of their language and alphabet.

Evans had identified three different kinds of Minoan writing. The first, and apparently the oldest, was a form of hieroglyphics, or picture writing. But these hieroglyphics were not like those of Egypt, which had been deciphered. Then there were two alphabetical forms. Evans called these "Linear A" and "Linear B." They were related, but the Linear B form was more widespread and more recently introduced; it was the alphabet that had been in use when the Cretan kingdom collapsed in 1400 B.C.

To decipher a language in an unknown alphabet one must first have some key, some guide to the meaning of the individual letters. Otherwise the inscriptions are just meaningless markings, and no amount of study can ever yield their message. Egyptian hieroglyphics were deciphered because of the discovery, in 1799, of the Rosetta Stone—a large flat stone on which the same message was inscribed in hieroglyphics, in ancient Egyptian business script, and in Greek. A French scholar, Jean François Champollion, tirelessly matched words in the Greek inscription with words in the hieroglyphics. After 23 years he had worked out only 111 out of the thousands of symbols on the stone, but it was a start—and, once the beginning had been made, it was soon possible to work out meanings for all the Egyptian symbols.

The writing of Babylonia was deciphered in the same way. At a place called Behistun, in Persia, the Persian monarch Darius had carved an inscription on the face of a cliff in Babylonian, Persian, and a language called Susian. Since the Persian was already known, a young English officer named Rawlinson matched it with the Babylonian inscription until he was able to work out meanings for the Babylonian characters.

But there was no Rosetta Stone of the Minoan language, no Behistun Rock. There was no place for scholars to begin the work, no foothold to be gained. It seemed as though Minoan would remain a mystery forever.

When Sir Arthur Evans was 84, in 1935, he lectured in London and told how the tablets he had uncovered at Knossos still defied every attempt at solution. In the audience was a 13-year-old English schoolboy, Michael Ventris, who decided to study the Minoan tablets and be the first to decipher them. It was an ambition he achieved—but it took him 17 years of work.

The Linear B tablets were the most numerous, and Evans had concentrated his work on these. Evans had been able to work out the fact that some of the symbols were numbers; this was easy enough, since they were simple marks that could be identified as problems in arithmetic. Evans also identified some 70 different "letters" in Linear B, though he had no idea of what those letters represented.

There are three ways of writing a language. One is by using pictographs, or hieroglyphics. In this system, a symbol is given to a *combination* of sounds. Thus there might be one symbol for the sound "pan," another for the word "man," and so on. This was the system in use in ancient

Egypt and also in China. It involves the use of hundreds and even thousands of different symbols, since the number of possible combinations of sounds is enormous.

A far simpler system is the one in use today, the alphabet. In this system, a symbol is given to *each* sound. Words are built up out of combinations of symbols. Thus, though there are many words, there are only a few symbols. The number of symbols, or letters, in an alphabetic system, ranges between 15 and 40, depending on the complexity of the language. In English, there are 26 letters, some of them unnecessary duplicates.

There is a middle way between the tremendous complexity of hieroglyphics and the simplicity of an alphabet. This is the syllabary. Syllabaries have symbols for the vowels, *a, e, i, o,* and *u,* and other symbols for combinations of consonants with these vowels to form syllables.

One such syllabary was known to have been used on the island of Cyprus in ancient times. Cyprus is in the Mediterranean, not far from Crete. In the Cypriote syllabary there are about 55 symbols. Five of them represent the vowels and the rest are combinations of vowels and consonants: *pa pe pi po pu, sa se si so su,* and so forth.

By the time Michael Ventris began his work, it was known that there were at least 88 characters in Linear B script. This was too many for it to be a simple alphabet, since there are not that many different sounds that can be formed by the human voice. On the other hand, it was far too few for Linear B to be a system of hieroglyphics. Therefore, Linear B had to be a syllabary system. Ventris suspected that it operated along the lines of the Cypriote system, though the resemblances between the two scripts were only superficial.

In Cypriote, every consonant has to be followed by a vowel. There can be no touching consonants. The name

Stasikrates had to be written *sa-ta-si-ka-ra-te-se*. And some symbols stand for several sound combinations: *ra* and *la* were written identically, since the language did not distinguish between *r* and *l* sounds. There were other special rules too. Ventris kept all these rules in mind as he began his work on Linear B.

The first step in solving the puzzle of an unknown language is to fit sounds to the symbols. Once the language can be pronounced, its similarities to other, known languages can be studied and correspondences worked out. But where to begin? How to guess at the sounds represented by strange symbols?

At first work went slowly for young Ventris. But then some surprising archaeological developments appeared. In 1939, the American archaeologist Carl W. Blegen, who had done important work at Troy, excavated the city of Pylos, ruled according to Homer by the aged king Nestor. Pylos was on the Greek mainland—and Blegen found 600 tablets inscribed in Linear B!

This demonstrated some sort of connection between the Minoans of Crete and the mainlanders, since they used the same form of writing. Some experts felt that this proved the idea that the Greek mainland cities had been settled by colonists from Crete. Others believed that the Pylos tablets might be in a different language from that of Crete, although in the same kind of script. After all, English and Hungarian are written in the same alphabet, but they are vastly different languages. They both got their alphabets from the same place—ancient Rome—but the languages are totally different from each other as well as from Latin.

Ventris suspected that the language of the Pylos tablets was indeed Greek, but written not in the familiar Greek alphabet but in Minoan Linear B. He was helped by a few rough sketches found on the Pylos tablets next to some of the words. One sketch showed a three-legged stand for a cooking pot. A three-legged stand is a tripod, or *tripodes* in Greek. In a syllabary system, that word would be written *ti-ri-po-de*.

By a combination of guesswork and brilliant deduction, Ventris worked out sound values for many of the Linear B characters found on the Pylos tablets. At first he was on extremely shaky ground, but soon he began to get so many Greek words that he knew it could no longer be coincidence. The Pylos tablets *were* in the Greek language, written with Minoan characters. But the words were an extremely old form of Greek. He got words like this:

Pa-ka-na
I-je-re-ja
A-to-po-qo

And they resembled Greek words. *Pa-ka-na* was close enough to *phasgana*, meaning "swords." *I-je-re-ja* was similar to *hiereia*, meaning "priestess." *A-to-po-qo* sounded like *artokopoi*, meaning "bakers!"

So far it might all be a wild coincidence, Ventris thought. But he continued to work out pronunciations for the Linear B characters, and when he pronounced the words, they sounded very much like Greek words. Then, too, he began getting some proper names from the tablets:

Te-se-u (Theseus)
E-ko-to (Hector)
Ko-no-so (Knossos)

Finally, Ventris came across a Linear B word of eight syllables. Applying his system, he read it as *e-te-wo-ke-re-we-i-jo*. Reading it according to the rules of the Cypriote syllabary, it was pronounced *Eteocles*, a familiar Greek name. From that point on Ventris was sure he was right. An eight-syllable coincidence just could not happen.

Other scholars, meanwhile, worked on the tablets as well,

concentrating on the grammar of the language while Ventris studied its pronunciation. They found that, grammatically, it was quite similar to ancient Greek, confirming Ventris' theory.

Ventris now went on to check his pronunciations by translating whole sentences from the Pylos tablets. He came up with good Greek sentences that made sense in English. One of the tablets read: *"This the priestess holds, and solemnly declares that the god has the true ownerships, but the plot-holders the enjoyment, of the plots in which it is laid out."* It was obviously a statement of some religious law pertaining to farming in Pylos.

Ventris' work was hampered because only a handful of the Knossos tablets found by Evans were published and available. But in 1951, Emmett L. Bennett, Jr., published the Pylos tablets found by his colleague Blegen, and the next year John Myres, Evans' successor at Knossos, published all of the Knossos tablets. Ventris now had the full range of Linear B inscriptions to work with.

And he made an unexpected discovery—the Knossos tablets in Linear B were also in Greek! Meanwhile, in 1952, a British archaeologist named Wace found Linear B inscriptions at Mycenae, and these, too, could be translated by Ventris' system.

The new finds raised new questions. Why were the Linear B tablets at Knossos in Greek and not in Minoan? An entirely new theory has arisen: that the Achaean Greeks conquered Knossos as early as 1600 B.C., and imposed their language on the Minoans. Certainly by the time of the fall of Crete, in 1400 B.C., the only language being *written* there was Greek, although both Minoan and Greek may still have been spoken.

Pots inscribed in Linear B have since been found in Syria, Palestine, and Cyprus as well as in many places on the Greek mainland. These inscriptions can all be translated into Greek through the system of Michael Ventris. So it seems that our theories about the relationship between Crete and Achaean Greece will have to be revised as the picture becomes more clear. Either the Achaean conquest of Knossos occurred a century or more before the earthquake that seems to have ended Cretan civilization, or else, for some unknown reason, the Minoans preferred to make their written records in the Greek language though in their own Linear B script.

Disappointingly, the translated materials from Knossos have not helped us much in our understanding of this enigmatic civilization. The tablets translated so far out of Linear B have concerned rather dull matters, just inventories of palace possessions and the like. We have found no poems, no plays, no historical annals. Perhaps these may yet come to light, and we shall learn the true story of the relations between the Minoans and the Achaeans. The business records so far translated are not very illuminating historically.

But there is also Linear A, the older script found at Knossos and nowhere else. Some of the characters of Linear A look very much like characters in Linear B; it seems clear that Linear B, *as a form of writing,* is a later development out of Linear A.

However, Linear A was soon discovered to be in a different language entirely! When Ventris' system of pronunciation was applied to the Linear A characters that resembled ones in Linear B, the result was nonsense. None of the sounds was remotely intelligible.

You must keep in mind the difference between a language and an alphabet. A language is a spoken means of communication; an alphabet is a symbolic way of writing down the language. One alphabet may be used to write many languages. English, French, Portugese, and Swedish are all written with the same alphabet. Russian, Arabic, and Hebrew all use different alphabets of their own.

Similarly, Linear A and Linear B were two related *kinds of writing* used to set down entirely different languages. Linear B writing was used to record Greek words. Linear A was used to record another language.

What other language?

Obviously, it was the original Minoan language. Only a relative handful of Linear A tablets had been found, and translating them seemed a formidable task. And, tragically, Michael Ventris, who might have done the job, was killed in an automobile accident in 1956 at the age of 34.

But other scholars worked on Linear A. In 1957, an American specialist in ancient languages named Cyrus H. Gordon, studying Linear A, applied Ventris' pronunciation to a pair of Linear A characters and found that they stood for the sounds "gab-ba." These are meaningless in Greek— but, Gordon realized, they were the sounds of the word that meant "all" in Akkadian, the language of ancient Babylonia! Quickly, Gordon worked out a dozen more syllables and proved that Linear A was indeed written in the Akkadian language.

But this raised a new confusion. Linear A was nothing like the script used in Babylonia. The Babylonians had had a complicated wedge-shaped kind of writing known as *cuneiform*, with many hundreds of characters. Linear A had less than a hundred characters, none of them similar to cuneiform.

So current archaeological thinking is that the Minoans, when they left the Middle East and came to settle in Crete, brought with them the language spoken in Babylonia. But they discarded the complicated Babylonian system of writing and invented their own. This we call Linear A.

Meanwhile, on the mainland of Greece, fair-skinned people called the Achaeans were building cities at Mycenae and Tiryns and Pylos and elsewhere. They spoke a different language, the ancestor of the Greek language spoken by Plato. Quite possibly these Achaean Greeks had no system of writing whatever. There are no written records of the Achaean era in the Greek alphabet. And in only one place in Homer is writing mentioned, a passage in the *Iliad* which tells how Bellerophon, an ancestor of one of the Greek heroes, was once given a written message to take to the King of Lycia. Bellerophon was unable to read, and the message told the Lycian king to kill Bellerophon when he arrived. But so heroic was Bellerophon that the King finally spared him.

This passage may refer to a message written in Minoan script. Almost certainly it was not written in the familiar "alpha, beta, gamma" Greek letters we know today.

Some time between 2000 and 1400 B.C., these two peoples came together: the Akkadian-speaking Minoans who wrote in Linear A, and the Greek-speaking Achaeans who did not write at all. Perhaps the Minoans taught the Achaeans how to write. The Achaeans used Minoan writing, changing it slightly to suit the needs of their own language. This is Linear B. Somehow, Linear B also became the writing of the Minoans, possibly after a conquest by the Achaeans. Then, in 1400 B.C., Crete was mysteriously devastated and the Minoans vanished from the scene.

On the mainland, the Achaeans continued to write in Linear B, for their inscriptions in that script have been found in levels dating after the fall of Knossos. When the

Dorians conquered Greece, they brought with them a new system of writing, an alphabet borrowed from still another race, the Phoenicians. The language of Greece remained the same, but Linear B died out and the Phoenician-derived Greek alphabet was used from then on for all writing.

Now that Linear A has been cracked, we may hope for a better understanding of Minoan history. Excavations are continuing all the time in the region, and perhaps some day we shall come across a document that will explain how Knossos fell. Our knowledge has come a long way in the six decades since Arthur Evans first began to dig in Crete. We now know something of the history of the whole Aegean area, and of the successive eras of Minoan, Achaean, and Dorian rule as well. Through a kind of brilliant detective work, Michael Ventris cracked the code of Linear B for us and showed that Greek was a written language on Crete for some time before its fall. The language of Homer's heroes can now be read from the tablets found at Mycenae and Pylos.

With far less to work from, Cyrus Gordon has solved the riddle of Linear A, the original Minoan tongue. As the work of digging and studying goes forward, more and more of the veils of time are being stripped away to reveal the history of these vanished civilizations.

4

Babylon

Human civilization was born on a flat, endless plain between the Euphrates and the Tigris rivers, in what is now the country of Iraq. Here, perhaps some 7,000 years ago, man's first cities rose. The area was called, in the Old Testament, *Aram-naharaim*—"The Land Between the Two Rivers." The Greek word meaning the same thing is Mesopotamia, and it is by that name that the ancient region is called today.

Two kingdoms arose in Mesopotamia. First came Sumeria, in the south, and its neighbor Akkad. These two countries, in time, became one: Babylonia. To the north, along the Tigris, a younger, more warlike people sprang up: the Assyrians. Under the Assyrians and the Babylonians, Mesopotamia was for a while the center of human civilization, even before the wonderful culture of Egypt arose. But, in time, the scepter of civilization passed westward to other peoples—to the Minoans, to the Achaeans, then to the Dorian Greeks, still later to the Romans, and centuries afterward to the wild races of Western Europe, the Gauls and the Huns who eventually attained civilization.

As time passed Mesopotamia by, the great kingdoms

crumbled and were destroyed. Only legends remained of the once mighty empires of the Tigris-Euphrates region. They told of fierce kings, of wise priests, of cities with incredibly lovely gardens, of towers that nearly reached the heavens.

Of all this, little remained except as told in the Old Testament, that record of a stubborn tribe of people who had suffered under the oppressive tyrannies of both Assyria and Babylonia. The names of kings had come down to us —Sennacherib, Nebuchadnezzar, Belshazzar. The names of cities survived—Babylon, Nineveh, Ur. But of actual works of these kingdoms, we had nothing. They had left no pyramids, no temples, no palaces.

In the sun-baked plains of Mesopotamia, wild Arab tribesmen roamed nomadically, and here and there a miserable poverty-stricken village had arisen. Strange steep mounds of huge size rose from the plain, but the incurious Bedouins paid little attention to them. The mounds had been there forever, they said. They had no interest in them.

But men of Europe, curious men, did wonder about those mounds. Could it be that the lost cities of Babylonia and Assyria lay beneath them? The Book of Genesis told of the Tower of Babel that had been built in the Mesopotamian plain: *"And the whole earth was of one language, and of one speech. And it came to pass, as they journeyed from the east, that they found a plain in the land of Shinar; and they dwelt there. And they said to one another: Come, let us make brick, and burn them thoroughly. And they had brick for stone, and slime they had for mortar. And they said, Go to, let us build a city and a tower, whose top may reach unto heaven."*

That passage explains the death of the Mesopotamian cities. The builders had had no stone on that silty plain. They had taken river mud and had fashioned it into bricks to dry in the sun, and had built their cities from bricks. But bricks crumble and must be replaced. During the long centuries of neglect it was not surprising that the once mighty cities of Assyria and Babylonia should have become shapeless, ugly mounds.

One of the first European travelers to suspect that the mounds in the Mesopotamian desert held the ancient cities was a brilliant young man named Claudius Rich, who, in 1811, while representing the East India Company in Iraq, traveled all through Mesopotamia sketching and examining the mounds. He went to one mound 25 miles south of Baghdad, a mound that bore the name of Babil, and found bricks with inscriptions in the then unknown cuneiform script. Of poor health, he was unable to make an excavation, but he did publish an important book, *Memoir on the Ruins of Babylon.*

Rich told how the whole countryside was covered with ruins. In some places, substantial fragments of brick walls could be seen. In others, the mounds were merely rubbish heaps. Beyond a doubt, Rich wrote, the cities of Babylonia were easily accessible to the digger.

One of the dreamers who read Rich's book was a Frenchman named Paul Emile Botta, a naturalist and the son of a historian. After considerable traveling through the Middle East to do scientific research, Botta got the appointment of French Consul in the town of Mosul, on the upper Tigris, in 1842. He was then 37 years old. Although no archaeologist, he had a scientific training, was accustomed to the hot climate, and spoke the native language. With these advantages, he set out to learn what he could of the lost Mesopotamian civilizations of long ago.

He began by going from house to house after his day's work, asking, "Do you have any antiquities for sale? Any bricks with old inscriptions on them? Old pots, old vases?"

He bought what was offered him, and asked where the ancient objects had been found. The natives shrugged and said, "They are found everywhere. One need only look."

So Botta went out to look. He selected a place at random, a mound called Kuyunjik at Mosul. But a year of digging there produced nothing but a few crumbled bricks and a couple of fragments of weather-beaten sculpture. In March, 1843, however, he heard that plenty of inscribed bricks had been found in the village of Khorsabad, 14 miles away. Discouraged by the results at Kuyunjik, Botta sent a couple of workmen over to try digging at Khorsabad.

Hardly had they begun to dig when they came upon two parallel walls of limestone, covered with sculptures and inscriptions. Bearded men, grotesque and weird animals, clashing armies were shown in vivid relief. And the walls were inscribed with the strange wedge-shaped writing that had also been found on the bricks.

What Botta had found at Khorsabad was a summer palace at the city of Nineveh, built by the Assyrian King Sargon II, about 709 B.C. As he removed the rubble, Botta laid bare a magnificent building whose courtyards had big gates crowded with sculptures. The entire life of this Assyrian civilization was depicted graphically on the walls Botta uncovered. But the limestone was fragile and crumbled quickly when unearthed. An artist named Flandin came from France to make sketches of the finds before they fell apart.

France was fired with enthusiasm by Botta's discoveries. Funds were granted to help him uncover the rest of Sargon's palace. But Botta had plenty of problems. Not only did his finds have an annoying tendency to fall apart under the hot desert sun, but also an entire boatload of statuary was lost when a raft bearing them tipped over in the Tigris. The natives stole the smaller pieces whenever Botta turned his back. And the Pasha of Mosul, thinking that Botta was digging for gold, set spies on him, threatened to arrest him, and put many obstacles in his way.

Botta persevered, and continued to unearth sculptures and reliefs that showed how the Assyrians had looked, how they had fought, besieged cities, killed prisoners. Their art revealed them to be a cruel, arrogant, warlike race.

Other diggers flooded into Mesopotamia to work at other locations, once the news of Botta's success reached Europe. One of the first was Austen Henry Layard, a Paris-born Englishman who was 28 when he began to dig in Mesopotamia in 1845. He had explored the Orient since the age of 22, living an adventurous life among the wild Persian tribesmen.

He had met Botta in 1842, and together they talked far into the night, both ablaze with the desire to rescue Assyria and Babylonia from their millennia of burial. But Layard had no money. Unlike Schliemann and Evans, he could not simply hire workmen and begin to dig. But his enthusiasm for archaeology was so infectious that in 1845 the British Ambassador in Mosul, Sir Stratford Canning, gave him £60—$300—to start him off. With this small sum, Layard began his excavations.

He planned to dig at a mound called Nimrud, near Mosul. But the Pasha of Mosul, who had caused so much difficulty for Botta, was equally troublesome to Layard. The Pasha was a Turk, short and fat, with one eye, one ear, and a face scarred hideously by smallpox. He seems to have been a despotic, villainous man, hated by all the people of Mosul. He taxed the people heavily, lopped off heads right and left, confiscated the property of anyone who dared to cry out against him.

Knowing the problem the Pasha had been for Botta, Layard decided to keep quiet about his archaeological plans. He let it be known that he was going to hunt wild boar on the banks of the Tigris. Carrying guns and spears to further this impression, he set off for the mound of Nimrud. On his first day at the site he managed to win the friendship of Awad, chief of the Bedouin tribe at Nimrud, and so was quickly able to hire six workmen at modest wages.

As work began, Layard became feverishly excited. The whole surface of the mound was covered with inscribed bricks. He hardly knew where to dig first. Chief Awad pointed to a slab of alabaster jutting out of the ground, and Layard decided to begin there.

His first trench turned up 10 slabs of alabaster within a matter of hours. It appeared to be the decorative inside sheathing of a palace wall. But the palace had been burned, it seemed, and the alabaster was cracked and fell to pieces when touched.

Layard let three of his men continue to dig there, and took the other three over to the far side of the mound. They dug there and soon stumbled over another set of ruins! Layard had found two Assyrian palaces on the first day!

The next day, five more workmen joined the operation. Palace walls came to light, similar to the ones Botta had found at Khorsabad, every square inch inscribed with cuneiform writing and superb bas-reliefs of battle scenes. Then one day an ivory fragment bearing a tiny scrap of gold leaf turned up. Chief Awad called Layard aside.

"Whatever you do, don't let these Arabs of mine know there is gold here," he whispered. "If they find out, news is sure to get back to the Pasha, and he'll make trouble for you."

Layard smiled and paid the chief for his silence. But somehow the Pasha came to learn that gold had been found at Nimrud, and even though it was only a worthless scrap of gold leaf he was immediately interested.

Slyly, he went to Nimrud and wished Layard well on his digging. But then he added, "You understand, of course, that this is an old Mohammedan graveyard. You are committing sacrilege here. I would not be able to protect you if the faithful worshipers attacked you."

It was, naturally, no Moslem cemetery. But during the night the Pasha's men dragged gravestones in from a genuine cemetery and planted them at Nimrud! Layard was stumped. He could not dig at the mound if it were a cemetery, and he could not prove the Pasha's fraud.

But while Layard pondered what to do, the Turkish government abruptly helped him by removing the Pasha from the scene. His misdeeds had caught up with him, and he was clapped into jail, his power taken from him. Layard visited the Pasha in a dismal room with rain leaking through the roof. "Thus it is with God's creatures," the ex-Pasha moaned. "Yesterday all those dogs were kissing my feet; today everyone and everything falls upon me, even the rain!"

There were no further obstacles in Layard's way. He dug again at Nimrud, and soon his men turned up a colossal statue of a winged lion. Layard wrote: "The gigantic head, blanched with age, thus rising from the bowels of the earth, might well have belonged to one of those fearful beings which are pictured in the traditions of the country, as appearing to mortals slowly ascending from the regions below. One of the workmen, on catching the first glimpse of the monster, had thrown down his basket and run off toward Mosul, as fast as his legs would carry him."

Word spread through Mosul that the bones of a Biblical prophet had been found. Layard was ordered to stop digging until the new Pasha could inspect the site. The Pasha came, was convinced that the find was a statue and not a prophet's bones, and permitted Layard to continue.

Soon he had 13 pairs of huge winged lions. The palace Layard uncovered was even more splendid than the one Botta had found. It was identified later as the palace of King Assurnasirpal II, who had reigned about 885–859 B.C.

While Layard and Botta were discovering the archaeological treasures of Assyria, other men were at work translating the strange cuneiform inscriptions that had been known since the seventeenth century. The pioneering work had been done in 1802 by a young German schoolmaster, Georg Friedrich Grotefend. Grotefend knew that there were three different kinds of cuneiform writing, which scholars called Class I, Class II, and Class III. Class I was thought to be the language of the Persians, who had conquered the Assyrians and the Babylonians in the sixth century before Christ. In later years, the Persians had stopped using cuneiform, which looked very much like bird tracks made on sand, and had started using an alphabetical system.

The New Persian monuments all began with the same inscribed formula: *X, great King, King of Kings, King of A and B, son of Y, great King, King of Kings, King of A and B* . . . and so on. Grotefend guessed that perhaps the Old Persian inscriptions, written in cuneiform, used the same general formula. He studied cuneiform tablets. The first word of the formula would be the name of the king, he knew. The second word would be the cuneiform characters meaning *king*. The same characters would be repeated over and over.

To his delight, he saw that there was indeed one set of wedges repeated endlessly, as though the inscription did read *great King, King of Kings, King of* . . . So he had a word. He also noticed that the inscriptions all began with one of only two names. So they all pertained to two kings, one the son of the other. He called these kings X and Y. Going farther, he saw that the father of King X was not described as himself a king.

So he had a beginning. He had *X king . . . son of Z,* and *Y king, son of X king.* Checking through Persian history, he could find only one grandfather-father-son set that fit this relationship: Hystaspes, Darius, and Xerxes. With this lead, Grotefend and others were soon able to decipher a great deal of the Class I cuneiform inscriptions.

While the scholars puzzled one letter after another out of the Persian inscriptions, a 27-year-old English major named Henry Rawlinson, stationed in Persia, was studying cuneiform on his own. Without knowing anything of Grotefend, he used the same method the German had, and worked out for himself the Hystaspes-Darius-Xerxes letters. But to go farther, he needed a lengthy inscription with plenty of names in it.

There was just such an inscription 20 miles from where he was stationed, at Behistun. Here, 25 centuries earlier, the Persian King Darius had carved an inscription in the face of a cliff some 300 feet above the valley floor. The inscription, legend had it, commemorated Darius' triumphs and battles. And it was in three cuneiform languages, one of them the Class I language of Grotefend, Old Persian.

An excellent athlete, Rawlinson climbed the dangerous cliff several times a day, until he had copied the whole Class I part of the inscription. A couple of years later, using long ladders, rope, and pegs for the climb, he copied the Class III inscription. It was very hard to get at, and he was in constant danger of falling to his death as he worked.

He knew of Grotefend's labors by this time, and it was relatively easy for Rawlinson to translate the Class I inscription, which began: *King Darius gives notice thus: you who in future days will see this inscription by order writ with hammer upon the cliff, who will see these human figures here—efface, destroy nothing. Take care, as long as you have seed, to leave them undisturbed.*"

Tackling the Class III inscription at Behistun proved vastly more difficult. By this time, the work of Botta and Layard had revealed that the Class III writing was actually Babylonian-Assyrian. The Old Persian inscription had been alphabetical in nature. Each symbol stood for a sound, just as in English. But in Class III, a single symbol might stand for a syllable or even an entire word. And some of the symbols seemed to represent different sounds at different times. Translating the inscription seemed hopelessly difficult, if not altogether impossible. The writing was just too complicated. For instance, the sound *r* was represented by six different symbols, depending on whether it was part of the syllables *ra, ri, ru, ar, ir,* or *ur.* And when consonants were added, to form *ram* or *mar,* still other symbols were used!

But a lucky find was made at Kuyunjik, Botta's first site. The "Library of Assurbanipal" was found—including almost a hundred clay tablets designed as instruction manuals for the use of scribes. Long lists had been compiled, showing how the old syllabic writing compared with the new alphabetic kind. Using these "dictionaries," Rawlinson and his colleagues were finally able to decipher the Class III writing, the writing of Babylonia and Assyria. And a Norwegian, Niels Westergaard, unraveled Class II, which was another Mesopotamian language called Elamite, or Susian. By the middle of the nineteenth century, there were many who could read the cuneiform writings of Babylonia and Assyria.

Other men came to work at Nineveh, the city that Botta

had located at Khorsabad. Soon much was known about the bloody Assyrian kings, all of whom took care to leave cuneiform records of their misdeeds. At Nineveh ruled insanely bloodthirsty kings, such as Sennacherib and Assurbanipal who conquered all the lands around, plundering and destroying. When Sennacherib conquered the city of Babylon, he left a boastful account of how he had dealt with it:

"The city and its houses, foundations and walls, I destroyed, I burned with fire. The wall and the outerwall, temples and gods, temple-towers of bricks and earth, as many as there were, I razed and dumped them into the Arahtu canal. Through the midst of that city I dug canals, I flooded its site with water, and the very foundations thereof I destroyed. I made its destruction more complete than by a flood. That in days to come, the site of that city, and its temples and gods, might not be remembered, I completely blotted it out with floods of water and made it like a meadow. . . . After I had destroyed Babylon, had smashed the gods thereof, and had struck down its people with the sword . . . that the ground of that city might be carried off, I removed its ground and had it carried to the Euphrates and on to the sea."

Now that archaeologists could read the Assyrian inscriptions, they saw the Assyrians for what they were: a race of soldiers, of destroyers, who created little that was original. It was apparent that their art and their language had been stolen from the Babylonians, the people of the south. Archaeological attention now turned toward the Euphrates region.

The first target was the city of Babylon itself, the capital of Babylonia. Babylon was known to be one of the most ancient cities of Mesopotamia, far older than the Assyrian cities of the north. About 1800 B.C., it had been the seat of the great lawgiver Hammurabi, and its origins probably went back a further 12 or 13 centuries.

There was little hope, of course, of unearthing the Babylon of Hammurabi. Even allowing for exaggeration in Sennacherib's account of his sack of Babylon, there could not have been much left of the ancient city when the Assyrians got through wrecking it, after their conquest of it in 689 B.C. But Sennacherib had fallen, murdered by his own sons, and nine years after the destruction Sennacherib's son Esarhaddon had ordered that Babylon be rebuilt.

The rebuilt city was ruled by one of the sons of Esarhaddon, but he rose against his brother and was destroyed. Later kings of Babylon were weaker, and in 626 B.C. a Babylonian, Nabopolassar, overthrew the Assyrian conquerors and proclaimed his city's independence. Under his son, Nebuchadnezzar, Babylon grew to become the most fabulous city of its time, until conquered by the Persians under Cyrus in 539 B.C.

It was this city, the city of Nebuchadnezzar, that the diggers hoped to find.

Layard was the first to make a serious attempt, in 1851. Finding the site was no problem. It had never been lost, and the mound, which had been visited by Rich forty years earlier, was still called Babil by the local dwellers. But Layard's investigations accomplished little. He found a few bricks inscribed with Nebuchadnezzar's name, some pottery, and a few late skeletons. But he found little else. "The discoveries," he wrote, "were far less numerous and important than I could have anticipated, nor did they tend to prove that there were remains beneath the heaps of earth and rubbish which would reward more extensive excavations . . . There will be nothing to be hoped for from the site of Babylon."

Layard was wrong. What he did not realize was that,

while the Assyrians had built Nineveh and the other cities of limestone, the Babylonians had had only mud to build with. In 1851, it was impossible for archaeologists to distinguish the mud of the walls from the mud of debris. Layard sliced through walls and rubbish alike, not knowing which was which. In the north, Botta, excavating the city of Ashur, was facing the same problem.

A new technique was needed, one which called for scrupulous examination and the most finicking kind of care. A "fine-tooth-comb" method of excavating was needed for the mud cities of Babylonia. A school of German archaeologists arose who specialized in this kind of minute detail work, and several of the minor Babylonian cities were excavated before the specialists felt ready, in the 1890's, to attempt the recovery of Babylon itself.

The man in charge was Dr. Robert Koldewey, born in 1855. A student of architecture, archaeology, and the history of art, he had had field experience in many parts of the world before he began the excavation of Babylon in March, 1899.

For all his methodical precision as an archaeologist, Koldewey was a light-hearted man with a sparkling sense of humor. So cheerful and waggish were his letters and reports that many of his colleagues did not take him seriously. But soon he began to uncover the city of Nebuchadnezzar, and other archaeologists started taking him very seriously indeed.

The Greek historian Herodotus had visited Babylon 2500 years earlier and had left an astonishing description of it. "In addition to its size," Herodotus had written, "Babylon surpasses in splendor any city in the known world." The great wall of the city covered a circumference of some 56 miles, was 50 cubits thick (about 80 feet) and 200 cubits high (320 feet). A hundred gates of bronze were set in this mammoth wall, yet it was only the *outer* fortification; within, Herodotus claimed, was "a second wall, not so thick but hardly less strong. There is a fortress in the middle of each half of the city; in one the royal palace surrounded by a wall of great strength, in the other the temple of Bel, the Babylonian Zeus."

The city, as Herodotus described it, was of such great size as to be unbelieveable. Most authorities had thought the old Greek historian had simply been telling tall tales.

But then Koldewey began to dig.

On April 5, 1899, after two weeks of work, he came upon the tremendous wall of Babylon. There were thousands of fragments of sculpture, of the kind familiar from the northern cities—winged lions, bearded kings, and all the rest. Koldewey removed tons of debris and exposed a brick wall 22.4 feet thick. Some 38 feet outside it, there was another wall of brick, 25 feet thick. And then something like a dry moat, with 12 more feet of wall beyond it. The space between the two inner walls had evidently been filled with rubble to make a pathway wide enough to allow two teams of four horses apiece to pass each other atop the wall. Every 165 feet along the inner wall there was a watchtower 27 feet high. Koldewey guessed that there had originally been 360 of these towers. The wall had been every bit as thick as Herodotus had insisted. It was not so great in circumference—Koldewey measured only 13 miles, as against Herodotus' statement of 56—but otherwise it had been described accurately.

And so Babylon had been the most solidly protected city in all the ancient world. Small wonder that they had built their wall that way, considering what Sennacherib had done to the city in his conquest. The rebuilt city, buried behind a wall 80 feet thick, was safe from any invader. When Babylon fell, it was not because the walls were broken, but because traitors within the walls conspired to let the Persians in.

The huge wall had been described by Nebuchadnezzar in a cuneiform inscription. "I caused a mighty wall to circumscribe Babylon. I dug its moats . . . at the edge of the moat I built a powerful wall as high as a hill. I gave it wide gates and set in it doors of cedarwood sheathed with copper. So that the enemy, who would do evil, would not threaten the sides of Babylon, I surrounded them with mighty floods as the billows of the sea flood the land."

Working within the walls, Koldewey next excavated the spectacular grand processional roadway that passed from north to south through the heart of the city. This titanic street, 73 feet wide, is perhaps the most majestic ever built in any city of the ancient or the modern world. It was bordered by massive walls, 23 feet high, decorated with brilliantly colored enameled bricks. Every 64 feet along the walls, lions were sculptured, red and yellow against a blue background. The road was built of brick, covered with asphalt and then great slabs of white limestone. Lining the sides of the road were slabs of breccia, a form of soft stone colored red and white. The edge of each slab was inscribed:

"Nebuchadnezzar, King of Babylon, son of Nabopolassar, King of Babylon, am I. The Babel Street I paved with Shadu slabs for the procession of the great Lord Marduk. Marduk, Lord, grant eternal life."

Along this street came the processions of the priests of Marduk, Babylon's highest god. Drums beat, flutes screeched, as the priests advanced, bearing the sacrificial animals, while thousands of worshipers followed. The effect must have been overwhelming.

But this huge street had another value besides the decorative one. It was a death trap for any enemies who might

107

manage to break through the 80-foot-thick walls of the city. The street ran from the outer walls to the inner citadel, and any enemy who sought to storm the citadel had to approach it along the Sacred Way. But there the enemies would be hemmed in by the high walls running the length of the street. From the top of the walls, the Babylonians could easily annihilate the invaders in a shower of arrows.

The Sacred Way led up to the Gate of Ishtar. Ishtar was the chief goddess of Babylon, and her gate was magnificent. Even today, the gateway stands almost 40 feet high, and it must have been far taller in Nebuchadnezzar's day. It was a double gateway, adorned by hundreds of brightly colored bulls and dragons. Today, the grand sweep of the Sacred Way leading to Ishtar Gate is breathtaking. In 600 B.C., when all was new and untouched by the harshness of time, it must have been a sight to make the traveler drop to his knees in wonder.

The Great Tower of Babylon was another of Koldewey's finds. The Bible tells of the Tower of Babel, which bold men built so high that it nearly reached God's throne. Each city of Mesopotamia had its tower, or ziggurat, rising in a series of steep terraces. Many archaeologists think that the people of the Tigris-Euphrates Valley originated in a mountainous region farther to the east. Migrating to the flat Mesopotamian valley, they built ziggurats as artificial mountains to remind them of the landscape of their first home.

The original Tower of Babel described in the Bible was undoubtedly such a ziggurat, and probably was built as early as 3500 B.C. By the time of Hammurabi, 1800 B.C., it was ancient, and was demolished and replaced. Then the new tower was pillaged by Sennacherib's hordes—but

Nabopolassar and Nebuchadnezzar restored it to its former greatness, and even beyond.

The Tower was the most sacred zone of the city. It was set in a great courtyard and surrounded by lesser temples. Each side of the Tower was 288 feet long, and the over-all height of the edifice was also 288 feet. The Tower rose in set-back steps, like a modern skyscraper; the first stage was 106 feet high, the second 58 feet. Then there were four stages of about 19 feet each, topped by a 48-foot-high temple dedicated to the god Marduk. The temple's walls were plated with gold and inlaid with blue enameled bricks, so that the sun, striking the top of the Tower, illuminated the entire city with a blaze of reflected light. Within the temple, a gold statue of Marduk and golden furniture were kept—according to Herodotus, 26 *tons* of gold altogether, an unbelievable fortune.

The Tower, destroyed by Sennacherib but rebuilt even more gloriously by Nebuchadnezzar, was not destroyed by the Persians under Cyrus when they conquered Babylon in 562 B.C. Cyrus was so fascinated by its splendor that he gave orders for his own grave to be designed in the shape of a miniature ziggurat. But a later Persian king, Xerxes, reduced the Tower to rubble during the quelling of a rebellion in Babylon. Still later, Alexander the Great, marching eastward to India, visited Babylon and put 10,000 men to work for two months, clearing away the debris and restoring some of the Tower's majesty.

There was nothing left of the Tower but the base, a great cube of crumbling brickwork, when Koldewey uncovered it again at the turn of this century. But the imaginative German could visualize the way the city had looked when the Tower still stood. He wrote: "The colossal mass of the Tower, which the Jews of the Old Testament regarded as the essence of human presumption, amidst the proud palaces of the priests, the spacious treasuries, the innumerable lodgings for strangers—white walls, bronze doors, mighty fortification walls set round with lofty portals and a forest of 1000 towers—the whole must have conveyed an overwhelming sense of greatness, power, and wealth such as rarely could have been found elsewhere in the great Babylonian kingdom."

A street, a gate, a tower—these were three of Koldewey's discoveries. The fourth memorable find was a garden—the Hanging Gardens of Babylon, one of the Seven Wonders of the Ancient World.

Koldewey was digging in the South Citadel, beyond the Ishtar Gate, and one day came upon a building with 14 arched vaults. It was unusual, both for the use of the arch in its design and because it was one of the two buildings of the city in which stone as well as brick had been used in the construction. At the western end of this arched building Koldewey found an odd well with a triple shaft, an oblong shaft flanked by two square ones. After some examination, Koldewey concluded that there had once been a chain pump in that well, with buckets on an endless chain fetching water and lifting it to the roof of the building. The machinery was long since gone, of course, but the design was clear.

Cuneiform inscriptions told of only two places in the city where stone had been used—on the north wall, and in the Hanging Gardens. This, then, had to be the site of the Hanging Gardens.

The gardens did not actually hang, of course. Actually, they were roof gardens, built high above the streets, and to the eyes of the people far below they had seemed to "hang."

Nebuchadnezzar, King of Babylon, had built the gardens for his young wife, a princess from Media. Media was famous for its fruits and flowers, and in rainless Babylon she missed the green hills with their fertile vegetation. So Nebuchadnezzar caused a series of terraces to be built on the palace grounds, balcony above balcony, to a height of 350 feet—as high as a 30-story skyscraper. Thousands of tons of soil were carried to these terraces, and trees and plants and vines were implanted there. An ingenious system of pumps brought water up from the Euphrates to keep the gardens green, and here the queen spent her days, reminded of far-off Media.

How had this wonderful city, with its Hanging Gardens and its huge processional street, its sky-stabbing Tower and invulnerable wall, fallen?

The Bible tells how Nebuchadnezzar went insane after decades of glorious rule, and died in 562 B.C. Babylon's decline began with the death of Nebuchadnezzar. He was succeeded by three kings within five years, each weaker than the one before, while the Babylonians abandoned themselves to drinking and carousing. By the time Belshazzar took the throne, a generation after Nebuchadnezzar's death, Babylon had been weakened by the conspiracies of traitors. Cyrus the Persian easily conquered it in 539 B.C. The Babylonians rebelled in the time of Xerxes, and the city was nearly destroyed in punishment.

After that, the decline was steady. The walls were in ruins, the great palaces shattered. Babylon lived on into the era of the Romans, but after the sixth century A.D. was inhabited only by peasants living in flimsy huts, and by the thirteenth century it was completely deserted. Desert sand and silt thrown up by the Euphrates soon covered the site of Nebuchadnezzar's wondrous city.

Assyria and Babylonia had now been uncovered by the excavators over a period of more than 50 years. But the cities that had emerged were fairly recent ones, and none of the finds was as old as those made in Troy or in Crete. Since it was known that Mesopotamian civilization was vastly older than those others, it was hoped that some really ancient cities would eventually be found. Were they lost forever? Had they crumbled into sand centuries earlier?

Babylonia and Assyria were relative newcomers on the historical scene. As the relics of Nineveh and Babylon and the other cities of the first millennium before Christ were studied, indications pointed to the existence of an older people from whom the Assyrians and the Babylonians had taken over their civilization.

In 1869, a Frenchman named Jules Oppert found cuneiform inscriptions of great antiquity in the southern part of Mesopotamia, that referred to an early ruler who called himself "King of Sumer and Akkad." Oppert named this early people the "Sumerians," and the name stuck.

The Babylonians and the Assyrians spoke similar languages. Their languages belong to a family of languages we call Semitic. Other Semitic languages are Arabic and Hebrew. But many things about the cuneiform writings of the Assyrians and the Babylonians argued that cuneiform had originally been the writing of a race that spoke a non-Semitic language. Somewhere in the past, this non-Semitic people had been conquered by the Semitic-speaking Assyrian-Babylonian civilization, which then adapted cuneiform writing to its own language in much the same way that the Achaean Greeks adapted Minoan Linear script.

But where were the relics of this unknown people that Oppert called the Sumerians? Would they ever be found?

The first breakthrough was made by Ernest de Sarzec, French vice-consul at Basra, Iraq. He was of the type of Botta and Layard—adventurous and scholarly, interested in Mesopotamian history, and willing to put up with heat and hardship to find the answers to the questions that troubled him. He dug at the mound of Tello, near Basra, late in the nineteenth century, and soon came across ancient relics of a kind no one else had found in Mesopotamia. There was the tombstone of a king called Eannatum, and statues of a ruler named Gudea, who had been king of an ancient city known as Lagash. The antiquities de Sarzec found were inscribed with thousands of cuneiform lines—but the language was a strange, non-Semitic one.

Were these the Sumerians?

Others came to dig at Tello, and then in nearby sites, and over the next 50 years the Sumerians came to light. Their cities were far older than those found by Botta and Layard. Some of the relics went back as far as 4000 B.C.—older even than anything found in Egypt.

Today we know a great deal about this race that existed at the dawn of history. The English archaeologist, Leonard Woolley, digging at the city of Ur, found the legendary birthplace of Abraham. He even came across traces of a great deluge that had swept Mesopotamia some 6,000 years ago—along with eyewitness accounts that left no doubt that this was the Flood of which the Bible speaks.

The Sumerians, we think, came out of a mountainous country, possibly India. They settled in the fertile Tigris-Euphrates valley some time before 3000 B.C. An even earlier race inhabited the region then, but the Sumerians conquered them. We know this not from any ruins that have been found, but because many words and names used by the Sumerians were not words of the Sumerian language. Just as such Indian names as Oklahoma and Connecticut tell of the people that inhabited North

America before the Europeans came, so do city names like Ur, Kish, and Nippur, which are not Sumerian words, tell of this earlier race.

But the Sumerians were triumphant, and built an important civilization in the valley. Their first king was named Etana, and he may have been the first man in all human history to build an empire. Sumerian influence spread far and wide. By 2500 B.C., they had developed cuneiform writing and began to set down the records by which we know them today.

They were a clever people. They lived by farming and fishing, and among their inventions were the wagon wheel, the plow, and the sailboat. They built complicated canals and reservoirs to irrigate their lands. They had measuring instruments, surveying tools, and the potter's wheel. They worked in copper and bronze, manufactured paints and leather, cosmetics, perfume, drugs. They had a well-developed science of medicine. All in all, they seem to have been a highly intelligent, ambitious, and capable race of pioneers, endlessly resourceful and inventive.

There were a dozen or so important Sumerian cities, some with 50,000 inhabitants. Each city had a great brick ziggurat, perhaps in memory of the mountains of the ancestral homeland, and atop each ziggurat was a temple dedicated to one of the gods. Their chief gods were those of water, earth, air, and heaven—Enki, Ki, Enlil, and An. They had myths of the creation of the heavens and the earth and man, and some of their stories may have found their way into the Bible of the Hebrews, who came in contact with the Sumerians.

They had sculpture, strange and highly individual. They had music. Harps and lyres were found in the tombs at Ur, and mention was made in their cuneiform writings of drums, tambourines, and flutes. We have discovered wonderful Sumerian poems, especially some that deal with the adventures of Gilgamesh, whose story is as fascinating as that of Odysseus.

This interesting and appealing Sumerian civilization, though, was darkened again and again by war. The cities vied with one another for supremacy. First the kings of Kish were dominant in Sumer, then Erech, and then Kish rose again, and then Ur. Gilgamesh restored Erech's supremacy, but after his death, Lugalannemundu of the city of Adab ruled for 90 years, the records claim, and his empire was vast. But a king of Kish named Mesilim overthrew him, only to be put down in turn by the kings of Lagash. One of the last kings of Lagash was Urukagina, who reduced taxes and gave relief to widows, orphans, and the poor. In one of the inscriptions of Urukagina is found the word "freedom"—the first time in man's history that this word appears. But when Urukagina had ruled 10 years, the neighboring city of Umma invaded Lagash and burned it.

This rivalry between the cities weakened Sumer and left it open to attack. A Semitic-speaking race from the west, led by King Sargon I, marched into Sumer about 2400 B.C. He built a new city called Agade and conquered nearly all of western Asia. The Semitic language Sargon brought with him joined the Sumerian tongue as the two languages of the region; both were written with the cuneiform script that the Sumerians had invented.

Sargon's empire lasted for a century. Barbarians from the mountains of Persia overran the cities, destroying Agade. Centuries of political confusion followed. It was at this time that Gudea, whose palace de Sarzec found, reigned in Lagash. But no one city could gain supremacy over all of Mesopotamia, and life was chaotic. Finally, a king of Ur named Ur-Nammu conquered Lagash and founded a new dynasty. He gave wise laws, insisting on honest weights and measures. In place of the "eye for an eye and tooth for a tooth" law of retribution that was then common among men, Ur-Nammu established a system of cash fines for crimes.

But once again Semitic invaders swept in from the west. One tribe, the Amorites, captured the Sumerian cities of Isin, Larsa, and Babylon. Ur was captured by a different tribe, the Elamites. All these tribes began to use cuneiform writing, but their languages were different.

For 250 years, the Amoritic kings of Isin, Larsa, and Babylon contended with one another for mastery over what had been Sumer. First Isin and Larsa, then Larsa and Babylon fought for supremacy. In the process, the original Sumerian people, conquered by wave after wave of invading Semites, were completely absorbed. Their name vanished from history, though their language continued to be taught in the schools and spoken by the priests for centuries.

About 1800 B.C., Hammurabi took the throne of Babylon. For 25 years he bided his time, until Rim-Sin, the king of Larsa, was aged and no longer able to lead his warriors in battle. Then the Babylonians struck, defeated Rim-Sin, and Babylon was supreme in all of southern Mesopotamia. In the north, the old kingdom of Akkadia, named for Sargon's city Agade, was invaded by barbarians who gradually began to build a civilization of their own as Assyria.

Hammurabi was one of the great lawgivers of history. He set down a legal code of 300 paragraphs, "in order that the strong should not oppress the weak, and that widows and orphans should be rightly dealt with." Under this wise and good ruler, Babylon extended its power to every city of the south. The region became known as Babylonia, after its most important city.

Sumer was gone from the historical scene now. Out of the chaos of the breakdown of the Sumerian Empire had come two new kingdoms: Assyria in the north, Babylonia in the south. Both spoke Semitic languages, and both had borrowed their system of writing and their technical abilities from the older, vanished race, the Sumerians.

The relationship between Assyria and Babylonia over the next 15 centuries was something quite similar to the relationship of Greece and Rome in the centuries before Christ. The parallels are striking. Just as the Babylonians had supplanted the Sumerians, the Dorian Greeks replaced the old Achaeans. And both new peoples had ultimately attained civilizations as high as those which they had replaced. They developed arts and sciences and sophisticated culture.

The Assyrians, like the Romans, began as crude barbarians far less civilized than their rivals. Gradually, both learned the ways of civilization: Assyria from Babylonia, Rome from Greece. But neither Assyria nor Rome had any real originality except in the art of making war. They borrowed their language and their poetry and their sculpture and even their mythology from the older race, and then ultimately attacked their mentors. Just as Greece eventually became merely a province of the Roman Empire, so too did Babylonia fall to the Assyrian legions.

From the time of Hammurabi to the thirteenth century before Christ, Babylonia was supreme in Mesopotamia. But about 1250 B.C., Assyria scored its first important military victory when Tukulti-Ninurta I, an Assyrian king, defeated the Babylonians in battle, and made their king a prisoner. A century and a half later, Tiglath-Pileser I had

117

made Assyria a fearsome nation, but his empire did not last. It was not until the ninth century B.C. that Assyria finally achieved complete dominion over Mesopotamia. First under Assurnasirpal (885–859 B.C.), and then under Salmanassar IV (781–772 B.C.), the Assyrians conquered Syria and all the lands down to the shore of the Mediterranean. Assurnasirpal built Kalah, the city Layard found.

Under Tiglath-Pileser III (745–727 B.C.), Assyria stretched her boundaries from the Mediterranean to the Persian Gulf. Armenia and Persia paid tribute to her. She subjugated a great part of the Kingdom of Israel. The next important king was Sargon II, who boldly named himself after the great conqueror of nearly two millennia earlier. He ruled from 721 to 705 B.C., and brought Assyria to the peak of her power. The bloodthirsty Assyrians killed and tortured for the sheer delight of the sport, terrorizing every neighboring city. At this time Babylonia was completely absorbed in the Assyrian Empire.

Under Sennacherib (704–681 B.C.), the insane son of Sargon II, Babylon rebelled. We have seen Sennacherib's own description of the terrible vengeance he levied on the city of Hammurabi. After him, however, his son Esarhaddon ordered the city's rebuilding, and went on to add parts of Egypt to the Assyrian holdings. But his descendants lost control of the empire. In Assurbanipal's time, Egypt regained its freedom, and the Assyrian kings that succeeded him were so obsessed with their evil pleasures that they let the empire fall apart. Under Nabopolassar, Babylon revolted and re-established its ancient independence. The magnificent new city of Babylon that he and his son Nebuchadnezzar built is the one found by Koldewey.

But this new Babylon was infected by the corruption that had flourished in Assyria for so long. Its splendor was

118

short-lived; its glory, though great, was founded on a shaky base. The city was sold by traitors to the Persians of Cyrus in 539 B.C. The Persians had already conquered the decadent Assyrians of the north. Those who had lived by the sword had perished by it. Soon the Persians abandoned cuneiform writing, which they had learned from the Babylonians and the Assyrians, for a simpler form of script. The cities of Mesopotamia dwindled to insignificance and the ancient civilizations were lost. By the nineteenth century after Christ, nothing remained but mounds in the desert—until Botta, Layard, and the others came.

History may not repeat itself, but certainly the vast patterns remain constant. In the previous chapter we saw how the Minoans built a great civilization, only to be overwhelmed by the Achaeans, who in turn fell to the Dorians. Each new society took what it chose from its predecessor, discarding the rest.

In the Tigris-Euphrates valley, cradle of civilization, the story was the same. First come the Sumerians, the first human beings to create a true civilization, conquering an earlier and more primitive people. Then, waves of Semitic invaders, ultimately submerging and obliterating the memory of the Sumerians. Two new kingdoms arise, Assyria and Babylonia; they make war, and eventually Assyria emerges the master—only to decay and succumb to a newer and stronger people coming out of Persia. And the Persians, in their turn, give way to the Macedonians of Alexander the Great, and on and on flows the remorseless river of history, through Rome and then through western Europe.

All this we know because of the diggings in Mesopotamia. From shapeless mounds have come the records of civilizations that were mighty 20 centuries before Troy fell, three millennia before Caesar and Christ. Behind all the later civilizations lie the discoveries made by the people of Sumer. As the archaeologist Leonard Woolley writes: "Their civilization, lighting up a world still plunged in primitive barbarism, was in the nature of a first cause. . . . The flower of genius drew its sap from Lydians and Hittites, from Phoenicia and Crete, from Babylon and Egypt. But the roots go farther back; behind all these lies Sumer."

5

Chichén Itzá of the Mayas

In the wake of Christopher Columbus the Spanish soldiery came to the New World, searching for gold and eager to spread the gospel of Christianity—if necessary, to convert the heathen at sword's point. The Spanish conquistadores found South and Central America already occupied by peoples who had attained a surprising degree of civilization. But the brutal and ignorant "civilized" Spaniards succeeded in destroying and uprooting, in conquering and shattering, these wonderful cultures of the New World.

In Peru flourished the Incas. The conquistador Pizarro dealt with them. In upper Mexico, the Aztecs were crushed by Cortez. Farther to the south, in Guatemala and the Yucatán Peninsula, a race we call the Mayas held sway. The Mayas did not resist the Spanish invaders as the Aztecs and Incas had, and so did not suffer so terribly. But they were conquered, and their proud spirit was broken by decades of slavery.

The Mayas had built mighty cities. The jungle was allowed to reclaim them, as it already had many others, long before Columbus. Year by year, the vines and shrubs crept more tightly around the buildings, until they were lost to sight—and forgotten for almost 300 years.

Today, many of the Maya cities have been reclaimed from the jungles. Of all of them, the most impressive, the most terrifying, is Chichén Itzá, in the upper part of Mexico's Yucatán Peninsula, which juts out like a huge thumb into the Gulf of Mexico.

We can visit Chichén Itzá today. We travel through the forests of Yucatán, and suddenly there it is, restored by archaeologists, the vegetation cleared away so that it looks once again as it did when the Mayas mysteriously abandoned it, in A.D. 1400.

The first thing the visitor sees is a great pyramid, crowned by a temple. There are 90 ladder-like steps to the summit. Scrambling to the top, one can see a stone palace set atop a terraced base. Just below it is the roofless Temple of a Thousand Columns. Looking another way, the vast stone stadium where athletic contests were held can be seen. Going still another way, one can see the observatory from which the Mayan astronomers studied the heavens. Smaller buildings stretch off in every direction, the ruins covering more than three square miles.

The great pyramid is the heart of Chichén Itzá. It stands 100 feet high, and in the temple at its top processions got under way—processions of death. For the Mayas practiced human sacrifice at Chichén Itzá. Maidens were sent to their death in honor of Yum-Chac, god of rain.

Down the steps of the pyramid came the procession—the priests first, leading the victim. A broad causeway stretched from the temple to a well a short distance away. Drums pounded and flutes wailed as the beautiful virgin about to be sacrificed was led across this causeway to the well. Hundreds of sacred images, in the form of feathered serpents, lined the edges of the road, which was 15 feet wide and a quarter of a mile long.

The procession halted at an altar in front of the well. The well was oval in shape, almost 190 feet across at its point of greatest width. From the brink of the pit, it was a sheer drop of more than 70 feet to the surface of the water. The well was another 60 or 70 feet deep.

Prayers were chanted. The terrified virgin shrank back as the strong hands of the priests reached for her. Trumpets fashioned from conch shells sounded a deafening fanfare. Clad in fine garments, decked in flowers, the little bride of Yum-Chac shivered as her death drew near. The drums rolled with a terrifyingly ominous boom.

Priests held the maiden, lifted her aloft, began to swing her. Out—back. Out—back. Again and again they swung her, in a dizzying arc.

Suddenly released, the girl shot forward, seemed to hang poised for a moment over nothingness, and then plunged downward toward the dark, waiting waters of the well.

There was a long moment of silence.

Then the dull boom of a body hitting the water, 70 feet below. The sound of a splash. Ripples spreading across the surface of the pool, and perhaps a few petals, ripped from her garlands at the moment of impact.

The sacrifice disappeared. The priests turned to one another and nodded approvingly. Yum-Chac was pleased with the offering he had received. He would smile upon his people. He would send rain!

For at least 400 years—from A.D.1000 to 1400—sacrifices were sent to placate the rain god whenever the priests thought it necessary. After solemn ceremonies, maidens were cast into the well, and after them rich offerings were hurled down—household utensils, statuary, golden plates.

Then, in 1400, the Mayas inexplicably abandoned Chichén Itzá. A population of nearly 100,000 simply deserted the city. When the Spaniards came, they found it uninhabited. Nothing dwelt there but snakes, bats, and jaguars. They made a few observations of the temples, took down some stories the remaining local Mayas told them—and then left the city to be engulfed by the jungle.

The story of Mayan archaeology begins in 1839, with John Lloyd Stephens. Born in New Jersey in 1805, Stephens was a lawyer by profession, but his hobby was archaeology. He visited Egypt, Arabia, Palestine, Greece, and Turkey, collecting the relics of ancient peoples. But when he was 31 he realized that he was overlooking a lost civilization that had thrived in his own hemisphere. One Colonel Garlindo of Mexico had published a report on certain great cities in the wilds of Yucatán. Garlindo's report happened to reach Stephens, who resolved to explore the region.

He set out for Central America in 1839, accompanied by his friend Frederick Catherwood, an artist and also an amateur archaeologist. Stephens managed to get the United States Government to finance his expedition, by wangling an appointment from President Martin Van Buren to be Special Confidential Agent from the United States to Central America.

Central America was then in political chaos, and Stephens and Catherwood arrived in the midst of a savage civil war. But they threaded a ticklish path through the rival armies, and set out on muleback for the village of Copán, in Honduras, where the road to the ruins began.

The forest was so thick they could scarcely cut their way through it. The trip was a nightmare. The pack animals sank into swamps; thorns slashed at the travelers; the heat was stifling; mosquitoes attacked in clouds. But they reached

Copán at length, and forged on beyond it into the jungle, accompanied by Indian guides hired at Copán.

Soon they came upon a wall built of stone blocks, hidden behind a tangle of thick vines. Ruins of a lost civilization? Or just an abandoned Spanish fort?

Within moments there was no doubt. With his machete, the guide hacked away the vines, and the two white men found themselves gaping at a richly carved slab of stone 12 feet high. On its front face was carved the figure of a man, his visage "solemn, stern, and well fitted to excite terror." The sides of the slab were covered with strange hieroglyphics, while on its obverse side were still other intricate carvings.

In furious excitement, Stephens and Catherwood slashed at the vines until 14 marvelous sculptured slabs stood in view. Two things were clear: that there had, indeed, been a race of builders living in these jungles, and that they had been great artists and not savages. Stephens sent back word that he had found works of art, "with more elegant designs, and some in workmanship equal to the finest monuments of the Egyptians."

They went on and on through the jungle. They cleared away the vines from a row of steps, climbed them, found themselves atop a lofty pyramid. They crossed it, descended onto a broad terrace. Other buildings lay ahead of them. The city stretched on "like a shattered bark in the midst of the ocean, her masts gone, her name effaced, her crew perished, and none to tell whence she came, to whom she belonged, how long on her voyage, or what caused her destruction."

An immense archaeological task faced the delighted discoverers. The forest would have to be cleared—a formidable job—and, since the ruins could not be removed, they would have to be sketched to show skeptics back home.

Stephens hired Indians to begin the monumental project of clearing the jungle. Catherwood set up his drawing board to make sketches of each building. He was bewildered at first by the alien shapes and proportions of the forms he had to copy. They were so unlike anything ever seen that he was hard put to sketch them.

Meanwhile, as Catherwood struggled and finally mastered the proportions of the sculpture he was drawing, Stephens forged ahead into the jungle. Wherever he looked, he found new pyramids, terraces, sculptured slabs. "We could not see ten yards before us," he wrote, "and never knew what we should stumble upon next. At one time we stopped to cut away branches and vines which concealed the face of a monument, and then to dig around and bring to light a fragment, a sculptured corner of which protruded from the earth. I leaned over with breathless anxiety while the Indians worked, and an eye, and ear, a foot, or a hand was disentombed; and when the machete rang against the chiselled stone, I pushed the Indians away, and cleared out the loose earth with my hands. The beauty of the sculpture, the solemn stillness of the woods, disturbed only by the scrambling of monkeys and the chattering of parrots, the desolation of the city, and the mystery that hung over it, all created an interest higher, if possible, than I had ever felt among the ruins of the Old World."

Suddenly a new figure appeared on the scene—a half-breed who introduced himself as Don José Maria.

"This forest belongs to me!" he announced. "I own this land where you are digging."

It seemed impossible to Stephens that the jungle could "belong" to anyone. But Don José was insistent, and finally Stephens, deciding that it was risky to start trouble in an explosive region like Central America, humored him. "All right," he said. "How much will you take for the ruins?"

Now Don José was taken aback. The ruins were worthless; he had asserted his claim only because he felt he was not being given the respect due a landowner. "My wanting to buy it," Stephens wrote, "seemed very suspicious."

Stephens quieted the half-breed's fears by showing him his credentials as a diplomat of the United States of America, and donned his brass-buttoned dress coat to look more impressive. At this, Don José agreed to sell. Stephens paid $50 for the ruins at Copán—and the natives thought him a fool for having offered to spend so much for a heap of worthless stone.

After working some months at Copán, Stephens and Catherwood moved on into Guatemala, and later into Chiapas and Yucatán. Wherever they went, they found other ruins. In 1842, Stephens published his book *Incidents of travel in Central America, Chiapas, and Yucatán,* telling the world of his discoveries, and illustrating it with a great many of Catherwood's superb drawings.

The book was an immediate sensation. It went through 10 editions in three months. It was translated into German, Spanish, and other languages. An unknown race that had lived in Central America, and built monuments on an artistic level with those of Egypt and ancient India? Fantastic! Remarkable! Who were these people, everyone wanted to know? Where had they come from? Why did they vanish?

There was a host of theories. No other Indian race had achieved so much, and therefore these jungle people could not have been Indians, some said. No; they built pyramids, and so they must have come from Egypt centuries ago. But others claimed that these people had come from India. Still others identified them as the lost Children of Israel, the 10 tribes that had disappeared from view centuries before Christ. No, said others: these Mayas were survivors from the sunken continent of Atlantis!

Others speculated that the Mayas had come from the

Pacific, or down from Alaska, or from ancient Carthage. But while the wild speculation was going on, a second Central American race was being rediscovered—the Aztecs of Mexico. William H. Prescott, in 1843, published his book, *The Conquest of Mexico,* which made use of forgotten documents left by the Spanish conquistadores. The Aztecs, like the Mayas, had built temples and palaces and great cities. Their language was nothing like that of the Mayans, but clearly they were a similar people.

Then, in 1863, a book called *Account of Things in Yucatán* was discovered in a dusty corner of the Royal Academy of History in Madrid. It had been written in 1566 by Diego de Landa, the archbishop of Yucatán, and apparently hadn't been opened for nearly 300 years. Now, at last, there was a first-hand account of these mysterious Mayas. De Landa is both the hero and the villain of Mayan archaeology. His villainous act was performed in July, 1562, when he collected as many of the books of the Mayas as he could find, labeled them "works of the devil," and ceremonially burned them in the public square of the town of Mani. In that bonfire perished hundreds of volumes of Mayan history and legend. Only three Mayan books escaped and still survive.

But, though his religious zeal led him to obliterate an entire civilization's priceless literature, De Landa was scholar enough to set down his own account of Mayan lore. His book included sketches of the hieroglyphs for the 20 days of the Mayan month and for the 18 months of the Mayan year.

De Landa's book was a vital find. Now there could no longer be wild speculations about the origin of the Mayas. A member of the conquering Spanish force had set down his description of the final days of Mayan independence. The Mayas, the world knew now, had simply been an unusually advanced Indian people. Thanks to the hieroglyphics De Landa reproduced, it became possible to translate the inscriptions on some of the Mayan monuments, and archaeologists began to take the first steps toward working out a history of the Mayas—a work that is still going on.

The next important name is that of Alfred Percival Maudsley. Beginning in 1881 and continuing until 1894, this Englishman ventured into Central American jungles seven times in search of Mayan ruins. He came out not only with sketches of Mayan architecture, but also with plaster-of-paris casts and paper rubbings of inscriptions, photographs, and even some entire sculptured slabs. His finds greatly increased the number of Mayan works available for scholars to study. Stephens, though important as a pioneer, had brought back little but word pictures and Catherwood's drawings; Maudsley returned with original material of tremendous value to archaeologists.

But the greatest individual contribution to Mayan archaeology was made by Edward Herbert Thompson, like Stephens an American, who spent 40 years in what he called "riotous exploration" of Central America. A New Englander who hunted Indian arrowheads in his youth, he came across Stephens' *Incidents of Travel* in his teens and was tremendously excited by his account of the Mayan ruins. Thompson wondered whether such sophisticated temple builders could belong to the same race of primitive hunters and fishers that were the North American Indians he knew. He decided that they could not. In 1879, he published an article called "Atlantis Not a Myth," in which he maintained that the Mayas had been a surviving branch of the people of Atlantis, that lost continent supposedly overwhelmed by the sea.

Thompson's article attracted attention, and friends made it possible for him to go to Yucatán in 1885 to conduct explorations. He was only 25, and had been given an appointment as a United States Consul. He thus followed the path of Stephens and Botta and many others in using a diplomatic appointment as a pretext to do archaeological research in a far-off land.

Thompson had encountered De Landa's *Account of Things in Yucatán* while preparing his article. One of the descriptions that most fascinated him was that of Chichén Itzá and its Sacred Well. Bishop de Landa had written: "A wide and handsome roadway runs as far as the Well, which is about two stone's throws off. Into this Well they have had and still have the custom of throwing men alive as a sacrifice to their gods in time of drought, and they believed that they would not die, though they never saw them again. They also threw in many other things like precious stones and things they prized, and so if this country had possessed gold it would have been this Well that would have the greater part of it, so great is the devotion that the Indians show for it."

Determined to find the Sacred Well of Chichén Itzá and to explore its depths in search of treasure, Thompson roamed Yucatán, learning the Indian language, eating their food, accustoming himself to hardship and privation in the jungles.

He hired an Indian to take him to legendary Chichén Itzá. They traveled for days, first by train, then by horse. The last leg of the journey seemed endless, and Thompson, plodding along in the saddle, was more than half asleep. Suddenly his guide cried out and pointed ahead.

"I raised my eyes and became electrically, tinglingly awake," Thompson said. "There, high up, wraith-like in the waning moonlight, loomed what seemed to be a Grecian temple of colossal proportions, atop a steep hill. So massive did it seem in the half-light of the approaching morning

130

that I could think of it only as an impregnable fortress high above the sea. . . . As this mass took clearer shape before me and with each succeeding hoofbeat of my weary steed, it grew more and more huge. I felt an actual physical pain, as if my heart had slipped a few beats and then raced to make up the loss."

Exhausted as he was, Thompson could not wait to explore the lost city. His guide settled down for the night and was soon asleep. Alone, Thompson scrambled up the temple stairway, overgrown with shrubs and vines, and breathlessly mounted to the top. He could see intricate sculptures, ornamented doorways. All about him were other ruins. Ghostly pyramids rose out of the darkness. Then he looked ahead, down to the raised roadway leading to the pool. This, he knew, was the Sacred Well of which De Landa had written. At that very altar, now half-hidden by the jungle, trembling Mayan maidens had waited to go to their doom!

The well was stagnant now, its water slimy, thick with the debris of centuries of neglect. But Thompson knew he had to explore that well. It was going to be a formidable job, he realized. Tons of muck and rocks and leaves would have to be removed before a diver could go down. And diving, in 1885, was a risky operation.

He returned to the United States to attend a scientific conference, and tried to raise money for his scheme of exploring the Sacred Well. His friends laughed at him. "No person can go down into the unknown depths of that great water pit and expect to come out alive," he was told. "If you want to commit suicide, why not seek a less shocking way of doing it?"

Thompson shrugged off their scoffing. He went to Boston and took lessons in deep-sea diving. He borrowed money and bought a dredge and a derrick with a 30-foot swinging boom. At great expense, he had this ponderous equipment shipped to Mexico and transported through the jungles to Chichén Itzá.

It was impossible to dredge the entire well, nearly 190 feet across. Thompson searched for the most likely spot by fashioning dummies out of wood, of the size and shape of a human being, and hurling them into the water. Thus he found the spot where the sacrifices had probably landed. He began to dredge.

Again and again the dredge, its steel jaw gaping, swung out over the water, poised a moment, and glided under the surface. The workmen strained over the cables as it emerged, jaws tightly closed over debris. "For days," Thompson wrote, "the dredge went up and down, up and down, interminably, bringing up muck and rocks, muck, more muck." Now and then a tree trunk would come up, the bones of a deer, the bones of a jaguar. A mountain of foul-smelling muck began to accumulate about the rim of the well. But nothing of any significance emerged. Thompson became depressed. "Is it possible," he asked himself, "that I have let my friends in for all this expense and exposed myself to a world of ridicule only to prove what many have contended, that these traditions are simply old tales, tales without any foundation in fact?"

On a bleak, rainy, discouraging day, the dredge came up with two round yellowish lumps of some resinous substance. Thompson sniffed them, cautiously nibbled one, then had the lucky idea of holding one over a flame. A fragrant perfume spread through the air. He had found Mayan incense! "That night for the first time in weeks," he wrote, "I slept soundly and long."

After that, hardly ever did the dredge emerge with nothing significant in it. More balls of incense came up, baskets that had contained them, a wooden knife, arrowheads and spear points, copper disks, bells, jade fragments, rubber balls and figurines, obsidian knives. Then the first human skull came to light, and after it many skeletons. The bones were identified as those of young girls—the many brides of the rain god Yum-Chac. Interestingly, one skeleton was that of a man, with broad shoulders and thick skull. Thompson originally thought that this might be the skeleton of some warrior sacrificed to the rain god, but later observation showed it to be that of an old man. Had one of the terrified girls pulled a priest into the water with her? Perhaps.

For months, archaeological treasures came from the deep. There were objects of gold now, particularly small golden bells that had been flattened with a mallet before they were thrown into the water. Many of the jade ornaments had been snapped in half—as though they had had to be "killed" before the rain god would accept them. The treasure of Chichén Itzá was not valuable in terms of money, Thompson wrote—but its archaeological value was enormous.

At last came the day when the dredge began to haul up splinters of rock, indicating that bottom had been reached. Now it was time to descend into the pool in a diving suit to recover the smaller treasures that had escaped the dredge's jaws. Thompson hired a professional Greek diver to accompany him. They rigged an air pump at the surface of the water and descended, wearing primitive diving suits made of waterproof canvas with big copper helmets, weighing more than 30 pounds, and goggles of plate glass.

It was a daring exploit, to descend in uncertain equipment into a dark hole such as that. When he was 10 feet down, Thompson found himself in utter darkness. Air pressure made his ears ache until he opened his helmet valves. Down he sank through the darkness. He wrote, "I felt . . . a strange thrill when I realized that I was the only living being who had ever reached this place alive and expected to leave it again still living. Then the Greek diver came down beside me and we shook hands."

They moved through muddy darkness. The dredge had cut a hole down into the mud. It was in this hole that they roved. Boulders were embedded in the walls of the hole, and from time to time rocks would work loose and plunge down upon them, knocking them over. The dredge had stirred up so much mud that their flashlights were useless, and they had to work by touch alone.

They felt their way along the bottom, until they came upon large smooth stones, some of them carved. Probing into crevices in the mud, Thompson found many articles of gold, copper, and jade. In one day alone 200 of the small golden bells were found. Then came a golden bowl nine inches in diameter, smaller ones, flint knives with handles of gold, embossed disks of gold—all the treasures the Mayas had hurled into the well during hundreds of years of human sacrifice.

After his successful exploration of the Sacred Well, Thompson went on to find the tomb of a high priest in a nearby pyramid. Prying up tiles at the top of the pyramid, he found himself at the entrance to a shaft—and looked down into the beady gaze of a boa constrictor.

The 14-foot-long snake was evicted, and Thompson entered the shaft. He found a heap of human bones. Lying beneath one of the skeletons was another loose tile, leading to another grave. Down and down through the pyramid went the succession of graves, five of them one atop the other, until he reached the base of the pyramid. There, where the pyramid rested on solid rock, he came upon still another chamber, this one carved out of the limestone base under the pyramid. It was filled with wood ashes, and when he cleared them away he found himself "in utter darkness in the bowels of the earth, balanced over a hole leading into who knew what depths and blackness."

"This is the mouth of Hell!" one of his native workmen cried.

"Not so," Thompson replied. "Since when has the mouth of Hell given forth a breath as cold as the wind that comes from this pit?"

Down they went, 50 feet straight down. At the bottom, a bead of polished jade reflected the light of his lantern. Jade amulets were scattered all about, along with fragments of a pearl necklace, and vases and urns. Below it all was one final tomb.

Clearly, this was the grave of someone important, at the very least a high priest or a king. Why else would he have been buried so deep in the earth, with a pyramid raised over his sepulchre? And why were there five other graves, one above the other, in the pyramid? Were these lesser priests who had been put to death when the high priest died?

Thompson had a theory which may very well be true. Mayan legend told of the hero Kukulcan, known to the Aztecs as Quetzalcoatl. Kukulcan, the legend said, had come to Chichén Itzá about A.D. 1100, an exile from the city of Tula in the north. The Mayas threw him into the Sacred Well as a sacrifice, but he did not drown; accordingly, the Mayas fished him out and gave him the rank of a living god. He ruled over them, becoming the most powerful chief in Yucatán. His name meant "feathered serpent," and everywhere in Mayan and Aztec territory statues and images of feathered serpents abound. Suddenly, at the height of his power, he disappeared mysteriously— promising to return.

The images of Kukulcan show him looking very much like a white man, and at least one portrait has him wearing a beard, while the Mayas themselves were clean-shaven. Some historians feel that Kukulcan may have been an actual white man, perhaps a wandering, shipwrecked Norse voyager of the time of Leif Ericsson, who established himself as a ruler in Central America. When the bearded Spanish conquistadores arrived in the sixteenth century, many of the Indians felt at first that Kukulcan had returned in fulfillment of his promise.

Thompson believed that the elaborate tomb he found at Chichén Itzá might well be "not merely the tomb of a great priest, but the tomb of *the* great priest, the tomb of the great leader, the tomb of the hero god Kukulcan, he whose symbol was the feathered serpent." Perhaps he was right!

The tomb also supplied Thompson with what he considered proof for his original theory—that the Mayas were survivors of lost Atlantis. No jade was then thought to be found anywhere in the Mayan territories, nor is gold mined there. The jade and gold objects found at Chichén Itzá must have come from other lands—and were obviously regarded as sacred. Also, the early jade pieces were quite large, but the later ones were small, as though the supply had been cut off and the Mayas had been forced to cut their remaining jade into smaller and smaller bits. Thompson theorized that the gold and jade had come from Atlantis—and when that continent sank, the mainland survivors in Yucatán had no more.

Are the Mayas Atlanteans? Thompson thought so. It is a fanciful but dubious theory that probably will never be proved.

Since Thompson's day (he died in 1935 after a long career of archaeology in Yucatán), extensive work has been done in the land of the Mayas. The archaeological problem is quite different from that in Mesopotamia, where ancient cities must be filtered out of millennia of mud and sand. The Mayan cities are quite recent, none of them much over a thousand years old, which makes them practically modern, compared with the 6,000-year-old cities of Sumer. And they are covered, not by mud and sand, but by jungle vegetation. The vines have pulled the temples apart block by block.

The work continues. The jungle is driven back, and temples and pyramids are exposed to view for the first time since the fall of the Mayas 400 years ago. In the late 1920's, Charles Lindbergh took aerial views of the ruins, and in 1930 a team of aviators made comprehensive maps of the entire Mayan region. Since then, archaeologists have carried on considerable work in the area. One of the major discoveries was made at Chiapas in Mexico, where the Mayan city of Bonampak was found, with three rooms of unique murals that gave us not only our most complete find of Mayan painting, but also a detailed record of everyday life in A.D. 800. Another important discovery was made in 1961, at Tikal, Guatemala, where a Mayan tomb of the year 457 was found—one of the earliest Mayan finds in such good condition. And skindivers working in Guatemalan lakes have made valuable finds since 1955.

More than a century of archaeology in Central America has given us a considerable knowledge of these Mayas. There are still many gaps in our understanding, but there is every reason to believe that these will be filled in as the jungle yields more of its secrets.

De Landa's book of the sixteenth century was the first important guide. It unlocked the mystery of the Mayan hieroglyphics. Three Mayan books had survived the burning of 1562, and these were in Europe, in scholarly hands. These Mayan books were written on sheets of paper made from pounded bark; strips of bark were joined to form books nine inches high and many feet in length, folded from side to side like screens, and painted on both sides. The finest of the Mayan books is called the Dresden Codex, which found its way somehow to Europe and was obtained by the Royal Library in Dresden in 1739. Since Dresden is in East Germany, the Dresden Codex is now being studied by Russian archaeologists.

The second Mayan book is called the Codex Peresianus, so named because the word "Perez" was written on its wrappings. It was found in a corner of the Bibliothèque Nationale in Paris in 1860. The third, the Codex Tro-Cortesianus, was found in two pieces at different cities of Spain and is now in Madrid.

De Landa's hieroglyphs enabled scholars to work out the meanings of these codices, which were filled with strange and colorful picture writing. We know now that the Dresden Codex deals with matters of astronomy, the Peresianus with astrology, and the Tro-Cortesianus with religious rituals. De Landa evidently burned the books dealing with history and myth, but not before he had recorded much of it in his own book.

One of the first things discovered with the aid of De Landa's book was that each of the many Mayan monuments was connected with a specific date. Everything was dated with extraordinary precision. The Mayas had an incredible obsession with time and its passing. They developed fabulously accurate calendars. Their entire culture seems to have revolved around this preoccupation with months and years —and everything is dated. The many mysteries of Mayadom would be even greater but for this bizarre com-
138

pulsion the Mayas had to mark the passing of the years with stone monuments.

The Mayas, we learned from De Landa, had two calendars—the tzolkin, or sacred calendar, and the haab, or true year. The tzolkin had 13 months of 20 days each, or 260 days in all. Each day and each month was represented by a design, or "glyph," of curious appearance. No one knows why the Mayas chose a 260-day year for this religious calendar.

The haab, however, was a 365-day calendar, as is ours. What is more, the haab was the best calendar ever devised —even more accurate than our own. It had 18 months of 20 days each, plus a five-day period at the end called Uayeb, the "empty" or "unlucky days." The actual year is about 365 days six hours long, and the Mayas, aware of this, periodically adjusted their calendar to account for this, just as we do with leap years. But the Maya calendar was even more precise than ours, by a matter of some seconds a year.

From this two-calendar system the Mayas built up a really complicated structure of time. 365 kins, or days, made a tun, or year. Twenty years, 7200 days, made a katun. After that came units called the baktun, pictun, and others, up to the alautun, which was no less than 23,040,000,000 days in length!

Still another Mayan calendrical cycle was a combination of haab and tzolkin. Once every 18,980 haab days, or 52 years, the haab and tzolkin cycles coincided. This 52-year cycle seems to have had some sort of mystical importance for the Mayas.

With this complicated system, the Mayas busied themselves by computing cycles far into the misty past. One Mayan inscription probes 90 million years into the past—

to a time long before it is believed that man himself had evolved! Their preoccupation with time exceeds anything known in any other culture.

The Mayan compulsion to date everything is a great help to the archaeologist. Of course, the researchers had no frame of reference at first. They knew how much time had passed between one Mayan date and another, but could not tell what the equivalent of either date was in our own chronology. For a period of over 1500 years, the Mayas had set up monuments with mechanical regularity to mark the passing of time—every 20 years in some cities, every five or ten in others. Also, the Mayas were content simply to carve dates into their stones. One slab found at Tikal is taken up entirely with calendrical information: "6 Ahau 13 Muan, completion of the count of 14, the completion of the *tun*," it reads. No data on the name of the city, or the ruler of the time, or on any historical event. Just the complicated date. To the Maya, dating was all-important and nothing else seemed worthy of recording permanently.

During the nineteenth century the *Books of Chilam Balam* were discovered in Yucatán. These were Mayan books composed after the Spanish conquest, written not in Mayan picture writing but in European letters. The language of these books was Mayan, and the transliteration into the Latin alphabet had been done confusingly, making decipherment a difficult job. But finally these books were translated, and yielded more information on the correlation of Mayan dates with our chronology.

Now we have some idea of the periods of Mayan history, though much yet must be worked out. There is still some controversy about the origins of the Mayas, whether they came from some distant land or whether they reached their high level of culture over a long period of evolution in their home territory. It is generally thought by many authorities today that the Mayas, like all other Indian races, entered North America through a land bridge from Asia many thousands of years ago. They crossed over from Siberia to Alaska, and migrated thence down over the entire Western Hemisphere.

Whatever their origin, the Mayas certainly were living in the area that is now lower Mexico, Guatemala, and Honduras by the year 2000 B.C. To the north were two similar peoples, the Aztecs and the Toltecs. One writer has compared the Toltecs to the inventive Sumerians, the Mayas to the cultured Babylonians who adopted the ideas of the older people, and the Aztecs to the warlike Assyrians who lived by bloodshed and terror. The parallel is not exact, though in many ways it holds up.

The Mayas of 2000 B.C. were a primitive, corn-growing, pottery-making people, scattered in small tribes all speaking the same language. We have only a few fragments of pottery as relics of this time. As the centuries passed they mastered the arts of architecture and farming. They perfected the loom to weave cloth. They spread throughout the Yucatán region. There was no central authority; each Maya tribe was independent. During this prehistoric period they developed their system of picture writing, which is the most advanced of any in the Western Hemisphere. (The Aztecs seem to have adapted it for their own uses: the Incas of Peru, on the other hand, never learned writing at all.)

The earliest known Maya city was Uaxactun, on the northern border of Guatemala, which was probably settled about the time of Christ. The earliest known date found at Uaxactun is A.D. 328, but the city probably is much older than this. Not far from Uaxactun, the temple city of Tikal was built, dating from 416. This is an immense city that has not yet been fully uncovered and is still being studied. It has eight huge temple pyramids, similar in design to the ziggurats of Mesopotamia. The biggest is 400 by 250 feet, and rises to a height of 229 feet.

The last date to be found at Tikal is A.D. 869. Was the city abandoned after then? Or did its inhabitants simply stop carving dates? No one knows.

Other Mayan cities followed rapidly in the next few centuries, until they spread all over the area. These were cities of stone, built for the ages. Yet they seem to have been occupied only for periods of a few centuries, then abandoned. There is no hint that these cities were conquered by enemies, or destroyed by natural causes. The Mayas, three million of them, simply left. Between 400 and 600, city after city was built and then evacuated, until by A.D. 900 the Mayas were heavily concentrated in the northern part of Yucatán alone.

Why?

Why did they leave these magnificent cities to succumb to the creeping jungle?

Perhaps the books burned by Diego de Landa might have told us. But those books are gone, victims of misguided zeal, and what we have of Mayan writings tells us nothing but a mumbo-jumbo of calendar computations.

The best explanation is an agricultural one. For all their cleverness at calendars and architecture, the Mayas were not good farmers. They used a system still practiced by Central Americans today, called milpa. In milpa farming, the jungle is cleared and burned during the dry season. Then corn is planted just as the rainy season starts. No fertilizer is used, and soon the land is worn out from repeated burnings. Then the farmer must move on, since the land needs to be left fallow for many years before it can be farmed again.

There is also a water problem in Yucatán. The land is

flat, and the topsoil is thin over an underlying bed of limestone. There are no rivers, no large lakes or springs. So even though the rains are heavy, water is constantly scarce. The Mayas built great reservoirs to catch the rainfall and store it against the dry season.

A city's life revolved around these reservoirs and around the cenotes, or natural wells. As the farmers spread out from one field to the next, they got farther and farther from their water supply. Soon each city was surrounded by a great stretch of burned-out fields that could not produce corn. Ultimately, the entire population of each city had to give up and move on to some other region, where they would build a new city and once again begin to farm.

And so the great migrations took place. The abandoned cities soon were swallowed up by the forest and forgotten. Some lay hidden for more than a thousand years, before archaeologists happened across them.

The curious thing is that it would not have been hard for the Mayas to develop irrigation systems. In Peru, where the coast is even drier, elaborate aqueducts were built to bring water over hundreds of miles. But the Mayas did not develop even the simplest of systems. They could have built water wheels to lift water from their wells, and then could have conveyed it by aqueducts to the surrounding fields. Strangely, the Mayas, who built such breath-takingly mighty cities, never mastered as basic a concept as the wheel. They used it only for children's toys, not for transportation or agriculture. They had no carts, no vehicles of any kind—and no water wheels. So they abandoned their cities, after farming the land around them to death, and moved on. It became too much of a burden to travel from the city to a field many miles away that was not yet exhausted. By their lights, it was easier to build an entirely new city!

143

Moving northward out of Honduras and Guatemala into Yucatán, the Mayas built new cities to replace Uaxactun and Tikal and the other abandoned ones. In 987 they built Uxmal, perhaps the most regular and beautiful of their cities. Here is located the House of the Governor, a stunningly impressive building 320 feet long, 40 feet wide, 26 feet high. It is covered with a veneer of 20,000 pieces of decorated stone, each joint inserted perfectly and carved with amazing elegance. A giant double-headed jaguar rests on an altar in front of it.

The greatest of the new Maya cities was Chichén Itzá. It had first been settled in A.D. 432, but had been abandoned, and was rebuilt about A.D. 900. By this time the Mayas had been met and penetrated by the Toltecs of Northern Mexico, who were attacked by the Aztecs. The Toltecs were absorbed into the Mayas, and gave them much that was new in art and architectural style. Another people, the Itzás, also migrated to escape Aztec ferocity, and they, too, were absorbed into the general Mayan culture. It was the Itzás who rebuilt Chichén Itzá in 964. Sometime in the eleventh century, the remainder of the Toltecs, fleeing their city of Tula, came to Chichén Itzá. It is at this time, the legend says, that Kukulcan came and was hailed as a god in Chichén Itzá.

It is the old story—the recurring pattern we saw in the Aegean with the Minoans, the Achaeans, and the Dorians, and in Mesopotamia with the Sumerians, the Babylonians, and the Assyrians. New peoples spring up, invade older ones, and either conquer them or are absorbed by them.

During the period after A.D. 900, the infusion of Toltecs brought a renaissance to Mayadom. New cities were built; new books were written. The character of life changed. The Mayas began to practice human sacrifice, now. The image of the feathered serpent dominated architecture.

Until this time, each of the cities of the Mayas had been independent of all others. A common language and common culture embraced them all, but there was political separation. In 987, however, the League of Mayapan was formed, centering around the new city of Mayapan. Mayapan entered into treaties with Chichén Itzá and Uxmal, and the three cities together conquered the rest of the area. Mayapan was a walled city with a population of about 25,000, and was undistinguished architecturally, lacking the ordered beauty of Uxmal and the monumental splendor of Chichén Itzá.

The League of Mayapan endured for many centuries. In 1194 civil war broke out between Mayapan and Chichén Itzá, and the latter city was conquered. Mayapan was supreme for the next 250 years. Then, in the katun, or 20-year period, called "8 Ahau," which ran from 1441 to 1460, Mayapan was destroyed. Fighting began within the city between two rival families striving for power, and, while this civil war was taking place, the Itzás (who had never fully reconciled themselves to being absorbed into the Mayan civilization) sacked the city. Its buildings were pulled down and its temples smashed.

The fall of Mayapan ended the unity of the Mayan people. Once again each city ruled alone, making war on its neighbors, as in the chaotic days of the decline of the Sumerian Empire. In such division there is weakness; the Sumerians fell easily to Semitic peoples out of the west, and the Mayas, too, were no match for their invaders.

The first white man to see the Mayas was Columbus, in 1502. He landed on an island off the coast of Honduras and met a party of Indians. When he asked them where they came from, they seemed to say that they lived in a place called "Maiam." The Spanish came to call these people Mayas, and their language Maya. We do not know, however, what they called themselves.

A later voyager, passing cities along the coast, landed and asked—in Spanish—who had built these cities and what the name of the country was. The natives supposedly replied, *"Ci-u-than,"* meaning, "We can't understand what you're saying." The Spanish took this as the name of the country, and turned it into "Yucatán," which was easier for them to pronounce. The Mayas had a different name for their own land, but we do not know what it was.

In 1511, a party of Spaniards was shipwrecked off Yucatán. They were found by the Mayas, who promptly sacrificed five of them, ripping out their hearts and serving their bodies at a banquet. Ultimately all but two of the Spaniards died this way. The last two, a priest named Geronimo Aguilar and a sailor named Gonzalo Guerrero, were thought too scrawny to be worth sacrificing. They were kept to fatten up, but broke from their cages and made their way through the jungle until they fell in with Mayas of a different tribe, who were less ferocious. Both men were made slaves.

Aguilar continued to say Christian prayers, and in 1519 he was rescued by another force of Spaniards under Hernando Cortes. But Guerrero all but became a Maya himself. He pierced his ears and inserted plugs, Maya-style. He learned the language and embraced the religion of the Mayas. Eventually he was released from his slavery and married the daughter of an important chief. He became a nacom, or war leader, and led his adopted people against other tribes, making use of Spanish military tactics.

The conquistador Cortes passed through Maya country in 1519, en route to his conquest of the Aztecs to the north. When he returned, five years later, news of his defeat of the fierce Aztecs traveled ahead of him, and the Mayas, terrified of a man who, with only a few hundred men, could topple the savagely warlike Aztecs, gave him little resistance. The land was split up into warring tribes anyway, which gave small hope of victory, since the Aztecs had been united and nevertheless had fallen.

Cortes encountered Guerrero, and was amazed to find that he did not care to be rescued. He was quite content with his new life as a Mayan chieftain. In fact, he proceeded to organize Mayan resistance to the invaders. Using their own tactics against them, the Mayas drove the Spanish out of Yucatán between 1527 and 1535. Perhaps, if Guerrero had not been killed in that year, there would have been no Spanish conquest of that part of Central America.

But Guerrero fell. With his death, Maya resistance crumbled. Some tribes surrendered at once; others held out, and were crushed with terrible brutality. By 1542, the conquistadores occupied half of Yucatán and had built a city of their own, Mérida. Four years later, the conquest was all but complete, with only one isolated tribe of Itzás holding out.

Now the conquerors set about to enslave the conquered, in the guise of Christianizing them. Priests who entered Yucatán in the middle of the sixteenth century, De Landa among them, took charge. The rulers were deposed, the priests of the Mayas executed, their religion banned, their books burned. The Maya chronicles say of this time: "Then began the execution by hanging, and the fire at the ends of our hands. Then also came ropes and cords into the world. Then the children of the younger brothers passed under the hardship of legal summons and tribute."

Half a million Mayas were made slaves. Every vestige of their culture was rooted out and destroyed. The Spanish were ruthlessly thorough, as their priests recorded in their accounts of this period. Luckily, they did take the trouble to write reports on the civilization they were destroying. Thus we know at least a little of this great race.

Mayan culture vanished with frightening rapidity. The Mayas had endured as a civilization for possibly some 4,000 years; they had been building cities when the ancestors of the Spanish were living in caves; they had had a mighty empire while Europe slumbered in darkness. Yet it took hardly more than a couple of generations for their culture to die. The Spanish had beheaded it. The books gone, the priests dead, the teachers silenced—there was no way for the traditions of old to be passed along to the new generation.

As we have said, only one isolated pocket of Mayadom remained beyond 1546. This was the tribe of Itzás who fled Yucatán and moved south, back to the ancient sites of the Mayan cities of 12 centuries before. They held on stubbornly, repulsing all attacks and executing any Spaniards they captured. They held out until 1696, when a priest named Avendaño reached their village alive and persuaded them to surrender peacefully to Spanish rule. In March, 1697, the Spanish occupied their village, and the last vestige of the independent Maya civilization went under.

The Mayas are not extinct. The blood of Kukulcan still flows in many inhabitants of Yucatán, Guatemala, and Honduras. In some villages, the old language is still spoken, though it is no longer written. But these survivors of today are peasants, ignorant of their great heritage. They know no more of the kings that ruled Uxmal and Chichén Itzá and Mayapan a thousand years ago than the wandering tribesmen of Iraq know of Sennacherib and Hammurabi. The Maya culture is dead, stamped into the ground by the Spanish conquistadores in the sixteenth century.

Thanks to the work of the archaeologists from Stephens' time to our own, we have recovered much of this culture.

148

We have cleared away the jungles, restored the temples, rebuilt some of the pyramids.

Yet the Maya culture is less known to us than that of the Sumerians who vanished 4,000 years ago. The Sumerians left us copious documents, annals of their kings, myths and poems, histories of their cities. The Mayas have left nothing but a mass of dates and three books. Even though their end came only a few centuries ago, we cannot name their kings, nor are we sure of the names of their cities.

But the work is progressing, and we do know a good deal about what sort of people they were. They were excellent astronomers, we know; they could predict eclipses, had mapped the stars, knew the time of revolution of the planet Venus. They were wonderful mathematicians, whose system of numbering was better than those of the Greeks, the Romans, or the Egyptians. They understood the concept of zero as a number, and so could perform vast complicated computations with large numbers. And their calendar, as we have said, was the best ever devised by any people.

The sculpture of the Mayas is one of the glories of human art. Their painting is fine. Their architecture stands out as almost unique. They may have lacked the secret of the true keystone arch and the secret of using the wheel, but they still managed to overcome these difficulties and build marvelous temples and pyramids.

They were a city-dwelling people who depended on agriculture, hunting, and fishing for their sustenance. Their society was divided into two classes, with an enormous gulf between. At the top was the nobility and priesthood, who called themselves the almehenob—"those who have fathers and mothers," those who could trace their ancestry. Their rulers called themselves halac uinicil, meaning "the true men," or "the real men." Below them—a long way below—came yalba uinicob, "the lower men," the peasants who raised the food, who served in the armies, who labored to build the temples and homes that upper-class architects designed.

The nobility lived splendidly. They were the ones who had the secrets of writing, who knew the ways of the gods. The "lower men" knew nothing but the daily round of toil. Thus, when the Spaniards ruthlessly butchered the almehenob, the aristocracy, Maya culture perished. The peasantry had been taught nothing but how to serve their noble masters.

The plans of the great Mayan cities show this gulf between rich and poor. The temples, the homes of the priests, and the dwellings of the nobles, all stood together in a plaza in the center of the city. These were the magnificent stone edifices that have survived today. They were built by peasant laborers, who contributed their services as a kind of tax levied on them by the nobles. Around this plaza of important buildings, the huts of the common people began, stretching out to the fringes of the surrounding farmland. These palm-thatched huts have, of course, not been preserved. But we can see from Maya carvings and paintings that they were of the same design as those built by Indian peasants of Central America today.

While the peasants sweated, the almehenob amused themselves in games and in intellectual pursuits. They must have been an awe-inspiring group, going about the city in their feather capes and jeweled armlets, with brilliant headgear made of the feathers of the tropical quetzal-bird. The "lower men" wore simple one-piece cloaks.

The Mayas had strange ideas of beauty. They flattened the heads of their babies by binding them between boards, so that the entire Maya race had an oddly pin-headed appearance. Because a squint was considered a sign of beauty, Maya parents hung balls of wax from their children's forelocks; the wax dangled back and forth in front of the child's eyes, eventually making him cross-eyed.

The Mayas had advanced musical instruments, most of them different kinds of drums and trumpets. They were a dancing people, and dancing was one of the important facets of their life; they had nearly a thousand different dances, performed at specific religious rituals. They also had the drama, and De Landa wrote of seeing "two stages built of stone with four staircases . . . and paved on top; here they recite their farces . . . and comedies for the pleasure of the public." These stages have been restored at Chichén Itzá.

A game called pok-a-tok was a popular Mayan amusement. It was played on a long, rectangular ball court the size of a football field. In mid-field, on either side of the court, a stone ring was set in the wall high above the ground—not horizontally, as in basketball, but vertically. The game was played with a rubber ball 6 inches in diameter, which was very light and bounced easily. The object of the game was to put the ball through the hole without touching it with the hands; it had to be butted or kicked through.

Pok-a-tok was taken very seriously among the Mayas. Enormous bets were placed on the outcome of a game. Sometimes the nobles played, and sometimes special teams that might be considered "professionals." At Chichén Itzá there are no less than seven ball courts. The largest one, built after the Toltec emigration, is 545 feet long, 225 feet wide. The goal is a stone ring decorated with a fanged snake; it is set 35 feet above the ground, so scoring must have been an extremely difficult feat to accomplish.

The Mayas are a fascinating people—a strange combi-

151

nation of genius and blindness. Highly sophisticated in some ways, bewilderingly ignorant in others, they are a people of many riddles. Because they left no history behind, we have been forced to guess at much of their life, and our guesses may not be right. We know less about the Mayas then we do about the Aztecs and the Incas—and we know far less about all three peoples than we do about the Babylonians and the Assyrians.

Yet work is continuing, and there is always the hope that a new Mayan book of chronicles will come to light in the jungle, hidden in some vase or urn at the time of De Landa, and forgotten till now. This is the dream of every archaeologist who ventures into Central America—that he will discover a scrap of ancient paper with the annals of Mayadom inscribed on it.

E. H. Thompson tells of one time when that dream nearly came true for him, many years after his exploration of the Sacred Well at Chichén Itzá. Speaking to a native about some ruins, he was told that the man had once come across a sealed vase in a jungle grave. Sure he had stumbled across treasure that would make him wealthy, the Indian hastened to open the vase. "But there was no gold or jewels inside," he told Thompson sadly. "Just a kind of paper."

Thompson's eyes went wide with excitement. "Paper? What kind of paper?" he demanded eagerly.

"Just a scrap of paper folded up," the native replied with a shrug. "It had what looked like a lot of little red and black monkeys painted on it."

Thompson began to perspire. Mayan picture writing included many signs that were in the form of faces in red and black. Was this a new find—a fourth Mayan book to add to the three already known? He grasped the man's arm urgently. "Where is that paper now?" he asked.

The Indian had taken it home and put it behind the altar. Where it was now, he said, only God knew.

"If you'll show me that paper, I'll give you a fine horse and a still finer saddle," Thompson promised. He hurried with the Indian to the man's hut. But no scrap of paper was in the vase. The Indian's wife remembered having thrown the paper away, one day long before, while house-cleaning. After all, what value could a paper scrap have? It just made the place untidy!

Thompson's disappointment was great, but archaeologists have to put up with this sort of tragedy as a daily routine. Still, hope remains. The key to the Mayan riddle may turn up next week, next month, next year—or 20 years from now. And then we may begin to understand more fully this unusual race of city-building Indians whose culture was smashed so ruthlessly 400 years ago.

Angkor, City in the Jungle

Imagine a city of over a million people—a city larger than San Francisco, larger than Cleveland, larger than Boston, larger than Minneapolis and Milwaukee put together. It is a capital city, like Washington, but it covers an area far greater than that city, and its monuments and public buildings are enormously bigger than those of the District of Columbia.

Now imagine this vast city abandoned—suddenly. The workmen lay down their tools, the mothers snatch up their babies, and all flee. The city is left deserted. For 400 years it stands empty, and the jungle creeps about it—the tangled, intensely thick jungle of southeast Asia. The city is lost to view. Legends of it remain, but the thick curtain of green hides it from the eye.

Picture, now, an explorer making his way through southeast Asia in the nineteenth century. He is Henri Mouhot, a naturalist whose prime interest is in rare butterflies. He is hacking his way through the jungles of the Kingdom of Cambodia, next door to Siam. The quest for butterflies has brought him to a part of the jungle that is completely unexplored. Swinging his machete industriously, he slashes away the vines and steps into an open glade.

He stares upward, rubbing his eyes in disbelief. No, he thinks. It is the heat . . . some tropical fever . . . some trick his mind is playing on him. For there, looming above the trees, are five titanic towers, so intricately carved that they seem to be festooned in stone lace. Living festoons of green vines twine about them.

To very few mortals is given an experience such as Henri Mouhot had a century ago. To stumble through the forest, to emerge in a clearing—and to behold a lost city of such splendor and magnificence as to dwarf anything known to man! Mouhot had found Angkor, capital city of a vanished race of Asia called the Khmers. The year was 1861. Angkor had been abandoned for 400 years.

But, in that first breathless moment, Mouhot knew nothing about Khmers, knew nothing about who had built this city or why it had been abandoned. He rushed forward, toward the towering piles of stone. It was an amazing city. Huge stone temples were silent in the death grip of strangling vines. Tremendous gateways, elaborate terraces, dozens of temples, miles of roads—all overgrown with lush vegetation. But, most surprising of all, it was in a perfect state of preservation. The clutch of the vines had been unable to topple towers or uproot paving stones. This was no ruin. This was an intact city out of yesterday, a fairy-tale city forgotten by time.

Mouhot forged on, into the city, making his way tortuously between immense silk-cotton trees and many-trunked banyans. No human voice greeted him. The only sounds were the screeching of birds in the trees, angry that a human should dare to invade their sanctuary, and the mocking chatter of a million monkeys clinging to the carved parapets. Bats whirred overhead; owls watched him bleakly from the tree tops. Snakes lay coiled on the path before him. Sleek panthers emerged from their dens and padded off into the dense jungle as the stranger approached.

Wherever Mouhot looked, he saw more temple tops jutting above the jungle. A complex network of canals and causeways could be seen, and moats and reservoirs ringing the great buildings. Mouhot roamed the city glassy-eyed with disbelief. Finally he staggered out the way he had entered, stunned and awed by what he had seen. He returned to the nearest native village.

"The city in there," he said. "Do you know of it?"

The natives nodded. They had come across it in their jungle wanderings.

"Who built it?" Mouhot asked. "Why was it deserted? When did the builders leave?"

They knew nothing.

"The giants built it," one man said.

"It is the work of Pra-Eun, king of the angels," another suggested.

Still a third, with a calm oriental smile, told Mouhot, "No one built the city. It has always been there. It built itself out of the trees of the jungle."

Today, a century after Mouhot's time, we know a great deal about Angkor and its builders. One by one, the puzzles of this lost city have been solved. Archaeologists, chiefly French, have cleared the jungle and restored Angkor to the appearance it must have had immediately after its abandonment in the fifteenth century. And, by studying the chronicles left by travelers of other nations, the mysterious Khmers have been made less mysterious.

We know that Angkor, or Angkor Thom (which simply means "great city") was the Khmer capital for hundreds of years. The Khmers themselves were the dominant people of southeast Asia for six centuries. Their first powerful king, Jayavarman II, unified the warring tribes of Cambodia under his control in A.D. 802. His capital was near Angkor, and in 889 King Yasovarman I built *his* capital on the present site of Angkor. Over the centuries succeeding Khmer monarchs enlarged the city, each adding his own contribution. Between 1113 and 1150 King Suryavarman II built "Angkor Wat"—"City Temple," the greatest single building of the city. A generation later, the capital was sacked by invaders called the Chams, but from 1181 to 1220 King Jayavarman VII reconstructed the city and gave it the form we know today. And, in 1432, Angkor was abandoned.

Those are the bare outlines of Khmer history. But we can also re-create their daily lives, now, as shown by the carvings in Angkor. The Khmers carved in their city as though a bare square foot of wall was somehow unlucky. They left stone portraits of their civilization everywhere.

They were basically a farming people, as are their descendants today, with rice the chief crop. They had a remarkable irrigation system, even more impressive as a technical feat than their temples. The surrounding countryside is threaded with Khmer canals and reservoirs. Some of the canals are more than 40 miles long.

They were mighty warriors, too. They had machines to hurl arrows and sharp spears to use on their enemies. They rode into battle atop richly decorated elephants. A Chinese chronicler of centuries ago tells us that the Khmers had fully 200,000 elephants trained as steeds of battle.

And they were businessmen. They traded with the other nations of Asia, particularly with China. They sold to the Chinese rhinoceros horn, spices, and kingfisher feathers, getting in return goods of porcelain, lacquerware, parasols.

157

Most of the Khmer records are gone. The peoples of Mesopotamia wrote on clay; those of Yucatán carved on stone. The Khmers wrote on hides and palm leaves and paper, all long since crumbled to dust. But their carvings tell their story. One temple known as the Bayon is covered with scenes of every-day life, photographs in stone. Between these carvings and the early Chinese chronicles, we can reconstruct Khmer life.

The Khmers began to develop their civilization about 2,000 years ago, under the influence of traders from India and later from China. A Chinese traveler of the third century A.D. reported, "The men are all ugly and black. Their hair is curly. They go naked and barefoot." A later account of the Khmer region, which the Chinese called Funan, said, "The sons of the well-to-do families [wear] sarongs of brocade. . . . The people of Funan make rings and bracelets of gold and vessels of silver."

In the middle of the sixth century, Funan merged with another Khmer kingdom inland known as Chenla to form a larger nation that called itself Kambujadesa—in its Westernized form, Cambodia.

Under Jayavarman II, the Khmers made themselves masters of a wide-ranging district. An Arab traveler tells of the fate of Jayavarman's predecessor. It seems that the young king of the Khmers was jealous of the ruler of another kingdom called Sailendra, in the area now called Indonesia and Malaya. "I have one desire I wish fulfilled," the young Khmer king said to his chief minister.

"And that is, O King?"

"To see before me on a plate the head of the King of Zabag." (Zabag was the Arab name for Java.)

Word of this lofty ambition reached the Sailendra king, who gathered an armada of a thousand ships and set sail for the Khmer kingdom. Marching to the capital, he easily routed the Khmer troops and captured the young king. He told him, "Your only wish was to cut off my head. You said nothing about capturing my kingdom or destroying my cities. So I shall do to you only what you would have done to me, and then return to my country. Let my victory serve as a lesson for your successors."

With that, he lopped off the young king's head and told the chief minister to choose a wiser man as the next Khmer monarch. The minister chose Jayavarman II—who succeeded in making Cambodia an independent and powerful country.

Jayavarman II moved his capital five different times, fearing invasion. Two of these cities were around the present site of Angkor; a third was at Mount Kulen, where the sandstone used in building Angkor was quarried. His final capital was back at the place that would be called Angkor. Here, two generations later, Yasovarman I laid out the city that was the beginning of the mighty Angkor known today.

He called his city Yasodharapura. He laid out an area covering six square miles, built a moat and a canal and an irrigation reservoir that was 4 miles long and 1 mile wide. The center of his city was a hill called Phnom Bakheng, where inscriptions praising Yasovarman I have been found calling him "The best of kings . . . unique bundle of splendors," and boasting, "In all the sciences and in all the sports . . . in dancing, singing, and all the rest, he was as clever as if he had been the first inventor of them." And: "In seeing him, the creator was astonished and seemed to say to himself, 'Why did I create a rival for myself in this king?' "

Yasovarman's successors enlarged the city, adding reservoirs and moats and new temples. In the process the city shifted northward, until Phnom Bakheng lay outside the city walls altogether.

In the first half of the twelfth century the great temple of Angkor Wat was built. Suryavarman II erected this huge edifice, the masterpiece of Khmer art. A moat 200 yards wide surrounds it. Then comes the outer wall of the temple, a mile on each side, with triple-towered gateways leading into the inner courtyard. An elevated stone pathway a quarter of a mile long leads to the main shrine. The pavement is deeply rutted by chariot wheels.

Angkor Wat is a man-made mountain of stone. Three terraces rise, topped with five towers, the tallest one 250 feet high. Galleries and courts stretch off for distances of half a mile in each direction. The holiest shrine is in the base of the central tower, where Suryavarman II installed a statue of the god he worshiped, Vishnu of the Hindus.

Everywhere there is ornamental carving, on every surface of this mammoth temple. The work is delicate and cunning, marvelously arranged. The most exciting carving is along the inner wall of the lower gallery, where, along a half-mile stretch of stone, gods and demons join in mortal combat, warriors and monkeys fight, monsters and humans struggle. These are scenes illustrating the ancient epics of India, the *Ramayana* and the *Mahabharata*.

The eastern gallery shows giants and demons fighting a monstrous cobra. In a panel in the southern gallery, Suryavarman himself is shown twice—once seated on his throne, in the shade of an umbrella, and once riding at the head of his troops in a parade to battle. His royal chaplain is at his side; priests carry an ark of sacred flame; an orchestra follows, blowing trumpets, beating drums and gongs.

All of these sculptured reliefs have a glassy sheen. They

have been worn nearly smooth by the hands of hundreds of Cambodian pilgrims who have come to Angkor in the last 60 years to see this shrine of their ancestors.

Angkor is easily visited today. Not so long ago, a traveler had to journey 300 miles by boat up the Mekong River, then take an overland trip of several miles into the jungle. Today, there is an airport 10 miles from the main entrance of Angkor Wat. At the town of Siem Reap, 4½ miles from Angkor, there is a hotel that runs tours of the lost city.

For all its size, Angkor Wat was not built to hold large audiences of worshipers. Rather, it was intended to be a symbolic home of the gods, and as the sepulcher for the ashes of the king. Suryavarman was buried there. Only a handful of priests ever roamed the temple's long galleries.

Not many years after Suryavarman's death, a Chinese mandarin was shipwrecked on the coast of Champa, a neighboring kingdom. For 30 years Cambodia and Champa had been at war, using elephants as their tanks. The mandarin taught the King of Champa the use of the crossbow on horseback, and in 1171 the Chams sent their newly trained forces against the Cambodians. A fleet sailed up the Mekong and attacked Angkor. The Cambodians fell before the Cham cavalry, and Angkor was captured and burned. The king was put to death.

But an exiled Khmer prince assembled an army and fleet, drove out the invaders, and made himself King of Cambodia, taking the name of Jayavarman VII. It was 1180 when he became ruler, making him a contemporary of Richard the Lion-Hearted of England.

Jayavarman VII was a great monarch. He lived for more than 90 years, ruling strongly and well. The earlier kings of Cambodia had been Hindus, but he was a Buddhist, and he built new temples and shrines dedicated to Buddha in Angkor and in the surrounding districts.

He was the greatest builder of Angkor. First he restored the parts of the city destroyed by the Cham invaders. Then he added buildings of his own. He put up massive new walls of stone to replace the wooden palisades the Chams had burned. He erected 102 hospitals, on one of which is inscribed: "He suffered from the ills of his subjects more than from his own; for it is the grief of the people that causes the grief of the kings, and not their own grief." He extended Khmer dominion to its farthest sway, and conquered the Chams, making Champa a province of Cambodia.

Jayavarman VII's greatest architectural achievement was the building of Angkor Thom, the new city, a mile northeast of Angkor Wat. Here rose his royal palace, with its fabulous pavilions and its majestic Elephant Walk extending for hundreds of yards along the Royal Plaza. In the center of Angkor Thom, Jayavarman VII built a temple called the Bayon, which is second in size only to Angkor Wat.

It is in the Bayon that archaeologists found the carved reliefs depicting Khmer life. It is a huge building, whose walls are rimmed with statues of giants and demons. The wall has five identical gateways of great size, and on each gateway tower are four sculptured heads, looking to each point of the compass. The faces are smiling—a strange, unearthly, unreadable smile, the "Angkor Smile," as mysterious as the smile of the Mona Lisa.

The Bayon itself is a warren of confusing galleries and passages, as much a labyrinth as the Palace of Minos in Knossos. Jayavarman VII built it on the foundations of an earlier temple, and his successors went on to add still more chapels and shrines, until the over-all effect became one of an unplanned maze. And on every wall are the carvings, a torrent of artistic energy expended in their creation.

There are battle scenes here—not gods and demons, but Khmers and Chams. The naval battles are shown in vivid detail. We see collisions between war barges manned by oarsmen and decorated with prows shaped like serpents' heads; we see crocodiles thrusting up their snouts to catch the dead and the dying as they fall overboard.

Farther on in the Bayon, less bloody scenes are found. Kings and priests are shown in their ceremonial robes at state functions. Nobles are portrayed watching circus performers do their tricks—dwarfs and jugglers and tightrope-walkers, acrobatic monkeys swinging from a pole. Other scenes show contests between wild boars, staged by the Khmer nobility for their amusement.

And there are humbler scenes, of women gossiping in the market place, of fishermen casting their nets, of men camping in the forest boiling a pig for their dinner. The Bayon's carvings show that peasant life of the region has not changed much in the five centuries since the fall of the Khmers. Ox carts much like those on the temple's walls can still be seen. Fishermen use the same sort of nets. The markets are no different.

Other Bayon carvings, of great archaeological interest, tell us how the massive buildings of Angkor were erected. Like the Mayas, the Khmers probably never knew the secret of using a keystone arch in construction. Instead, they built their temples the hard way, flat stone upon flat stone without an archway. The sandstone building blocks were quarried 25 miles from Angkor and dragged to the city by teams of elephants. Workmen drilled holes in the blocks and set pegs in them to aid in handling. Using rope and pulleys, they lifted the blocks, set them in place, and ground them back and forth until they fitted perfectly over

163

the ones beneath. The Khmers used no mortar to hold their constructions together. To build the higher galleries, they erected scaffolds of bamboo.

The colossal building accomplishments of Jayavarman VII ended the great phase of Angkor's history. After his death in 1220, later kings added little to the city, simply maintaining what was already there. Jayavarman VII built not only in Angkor but also beyond; the entire district is studded with shrines and bridges and roads, some of which have not yet been freed of jungle entrapments. One of the greatest of these outlying buildings is the monastery of Ta Prohm, built by Jayavarman VII as a shrine to his mother. It still is in the jungle's grip, but one inscription has been uncovered that says that the monastery had 18 high priests and 2,740 ordinary priests, who were aided in the ceremonies by 2,232 assistants, including 615 women dancers. As many as 12,640 people were said to have lived in the monastery, and 66,625 lived nearby to supply it with food and services—nearly 80,000 Khmers attached to a single monastery!

The thirteenth and the fourteenth centuries were years of decline for Angkor and the entire Khmer Empire. The kings were content to live in the splendid cities built by their ancestors. Life was soft. Other races grew strong in the outlying districts—the Thai, the Lao, the Annamese.

Marco Polo, roaming Asia, came close to Cambodia in the late thirteenth century. He visited coastal Champa, and had he penetrated inland he might have been able to tell of Angkor, along with the other wonders of which he wrote. But he never saw the great Khmer city. One traveler who did was a Chinese merchant named Chou Ta-kuan, who spent 11 months there in 1296–97, and wrote a detailed account of his visit.

Chou Ta-kuan told of the Bayon, describing it as

shining with gold. "On the eastern side is a golden bridge, on each side of which are two golden lions, while eight golden Buddhas are placed at the base of the stone chambers." He also recorded Khmer myths. Speaking of a small palace called the Phimeanakas, he wrote: "In the tower dwells the spirit of a nine-headed serpent, who is master of the soil of the whole kingdom. It appears every night in the form of a woman, and the king goes to her. . . . If one night the spirit of this serpent does not appear, then the king's time has come to die. If the king fails to come for a single night, some misfortune will happen to him."

Chou was unable to describe the inside of the royal palaces. He says, "I have heard that inside the palace are many marvelous places, but there are very severe restrictions, and it is impossible to enter." But he told how the king appeared twice a day at a golden window of the palace, to dispense justice to the people. He wrote of the New Year's celebrations, when firework displays were held for two weeks' time. He praised the women of the palace, writing that the king had 3,000 to 5,000 wives and concubines, "many as light as jade."

As the enemies of the Khmers grew stronger, the Khmers themselves grew less able to defend themselves. Some writers even believe that the many building projects of Jayavarman VII so exhausted the people of Cambodia that they began to decline after his death from sheer cultural fatigue. Again and again, the Annamese and the Thais raided Cambodian territory. The Khmers, who had once been Hindus, were converted to the gentler religion of Buddhism, and were less eager to distinguish themselves in battle.

In 1431, the Thais, whose kingdom, northwest of Cambodia, was once known as Siam and is now again called Thailand, laid siege to Angkor. For seven months the walled city held out, but finally it surrendered. The Thai armies entered the city, looting and burning. They carried off priests, artists, dancers, and sculptors to their own capital, and thus many Cambodian styles of art and dance were transplanted to Thailand. The Thais also set up a puppet government of their own in Angkor.

In 1432, the Khmers rebelled against the Thai overlords and drove them out. But the restored Khmer king, Pona Yat, decided that the splendid capital was too close to enemy territory, too hard to defend. He moved his court south, beyond the great lake called Tonle Sap, and established a new city, Phnom Penh, which is still the capital of Cambodia today.

And so Angkor was abandoned by its builders. Perhaps it was occupied by Thais for a few years, but they must have felt oppressed by the size and majesty of this city, and they left it to the bats and the snakes and to the encroaching jungle vines. Within a generation, possibly, Angkor was swallowed up by the jungle.

Cambodia survived as an independent nation, though under constant harassment by Thais and Annamese, who conquered much of its territory. In the 1860's, the French established a protectorate over the entire region except for Thailand, calling it French Indochina. It was during French dominance here that Mouhot found Angkor, and it was while the French governed that archaeologists from Paris performed the great task of freeing Angkor from the grip of the jungle.

After World War II, the peoples of Indochina fought for their liberation from French rule, and in 1954 the French withdrew. What had been French Indochina was divided into four states: Cambodia, Laos, and North and South Viet Nam. Since then, the area has become a battleground between the forces of Communism and the West. North

Viet Nam and part of Laos are under Communist rule as this book is written; Cambodia is still maintaining its freedom. And in the part of Cambodia where the remnants of the Khmer cities are found, American bulldozers and ditchdiggers are being used to rebuild the old reservoirs and to re-establish the miraculous irrigation networks of the Khmers.

The descendants of the Khmers are the people of today's Cambodia, and some of them, mindful of their past, call themselves Khmers too. Just as in Central America there still are Indians who are known as Mayas, in Cambodia there are those who think of themselves as Khmers.

But the Khmer civilization passed away in the fifteenth century. They dominated southeast Asia from A.D. 800 on, they built their stupendous stone cities, and, when their time came to depart, they faded into insignificance. In his book *The Ancient Khmer Empire,* Lawrence Palmer Briggs writes: "The Khmers left the world no great systems of administration, education, or ethics, like those of China; no literatures, religions, or systems of philosophy, like those of India; but here Oriental architecture and decoration reached its culminating point."

The Khmer temples and pyramids stand yet, to remind us of the glories of this bygone people. The lucky find of Henri Mouhot, and the work of the archaeologists who followed him, have given us a city whose every building is a poem in stone, a city of unsurpassable beauty, whose like the world may never see again.

Epilogue

And so we have visited six civilizations of yesterday, have seen them rise and fall, have seen the world forget them, have watched them rediscovered. The end came swiftly at Pompeii, where a city died in a single day. In Crete, too, the final conquest must have been a rapid one. A single generation was enough to make an end to the Mayan culture, a year or two to see Angkor deserted, one great war sufficient to end Troy's reign. Only in Mesopotamia was the process a slow one of decline and ultimate subjugation.

The science of archaeology has given these lands of yesterday back to us. Men with spades and shovels, with machetes and hacksaws, have freed these cities from the grip of oblivion. We know something of our past now. We have brought dead languages to life. Kings who flourished millennia ago are known to us.

But the work of archaeology never ends. In the "inner space" below the surface of the earth, still more secrets remain hidden, other civilizations still pose riddles. Throughout the world men are at work as this book is being read. In Mesopotamia, in Egypt, in Greece, in Italy,

169

in Crete, in Cambodia—in a hundred sites where men have dwelt. There are other races of whom we know little and thirst to know more—the Etruscans who ruled in Italy before Rome, the Hittites of Western Asia, the ancient Dravidians of India. The archaeology of Africa has only just begun. There is much yet to do.

We have seen how the great archaeologists—Schliemann and Evans and Layard and the rest—began their careers by reading of what had gone before. Who knows but that the Schliemanns and the Layards of today, still going to school, are destined to make the archaeological discoveries that will ring through the decades to come? What mysteries will be solved in 1980 or 1990 by future archaeologists now in their teens or even younger?

And a fabulous prospect is opening before us as man thrusts into outer space. Before many years pass, men will walk the surface of the moon. After that, it cannot be long before we reach the nearby planets, Mars, Venus.

Today we think that no intelligent peoples live on those planets. We may be wrong. Or, possibly, mighty races flourished there hundreds of centuries ago, built their kingdoms and empires, and died out. The deserts of Mars may be as fertile for archaeologists as those of Mesopotamia have been. Instead of one world's past to explore, there may be two or three planets whose past cries out to be recaptured.

Who knows but that the Schliemann of Mars has already been born? Who knows what wonders will greet his eyes 40 years hence.

Who knows?

For Further Reading

This book is only an introduction to a few of the many civilizations uncovered by archaeology. In the brief chapters no more than the bare bones of each story have been set down.

Each chapter of this book could have been a book in itself, and indeed many, many whole books have been written about each of the six vanished civilizations. Here, for the reader who wants to learn about these civilizations in detail, I append a list of books that will be useful. Some are in print; others are old and hard to find, but may be available in the libraries of larger cities.

POMPEII

The Destruction and Resurrection of Pompeii and Herculaneum, by E. C. C. Corti. Routledge & Kegan Paul, London, 1951.

Pompeii, by R. C. Carrington. Clarendon Press, Oxford, 1936.

The Common People of Pompeii, by Helen Tanzer. Johns Hopkins Press, Baltimore, 1937.

Pompeii and Its Tragedy, by Luigi Confalonieri. Aldo Martello Editore, Milan, 1959. (Available in an English translation.)

TROY

Troy, by Carl W. Blegen. Princeton University Press, Princeton, 1952.

Schliemann; the Story of a Gold-Seeker, by Emil Ludwig. Boston, 1931.

Ilios, by Heinrich Schliemann. New York, 1881.

CRETE

The Bull of Minos, by Leonard Cottrell. Pan Books, London, 1955 (revised edition).

The Palace of Minos, by Sir Arthur Evans. Macmillan, London. Four volumes, 1921–35.

Time and Chance, by Joan Evans. Longmans Green, London, 1943.

The Sea-Kings of Crete, by James Baikie. London, 1926.

MESOPOTAMIA

Nineveh and Its Remains, by A. H. Layard. New York, 1853.

Digging Up the Past, by Sir Charles Leonard Woolley. Crowell, New York, 1954.

Ur of the Chaldees, by Sir Charles Leonard Woolley. Penguin Books, London, 1940.

The Birth of Civilization in the Near East, by Henri Frankfort. Doubleday, New York, 1956.

Before Philosophy, by H. Frankfort, etc. Penguin Books, London, 1949.

THE MAYAS

Discoveries and Adventures in Central America, by Thomas Gann. London, 1928.

Yucatán Before and After the Conquest, with Other Related Documents, by Bishop Diego de Landa. Translated with notes by William Gates. Baltimore, 1937.

Incidents of Travel in Central America, Chiapas, and Yucatán, by John Lloyd Stephens. New York, 1841.

People of the Serpent, by E. H. Thompson. New York, 1932.

The City of the Sacred Well, by Theodore Arthur Willard. New York, 1926.

World of the Maya, by Victor W. von Hagen. Mentor Books, New York, 1960.

ANGKOR

Travels in Indo-China, by A. H. Mouhot. London, 1864.

Angkor the Magnificent, by H. C. Candee. New York, 1925.

GENERAL

Gods, Graves, and Scholars, by C. W. Ceram. Knopf, New York, 1951.

Beginnings in Archaeology, by K. M. Kenyon. Praeger, New York, 1953.

Archaeology from the Earth, by Sir Morton Wheeler. Clarendon Press, Oxford, 1954.

The Anvil of Civilization, by Leonard Cottrell. Mentor Books, New York, 1957.

Index

176